"It seems so frequent now that we hear about shootings taking place again and again. And yet, each time we ask: why does this continue to happen? Unfortunately, many of us are not equipped to discuss gun violence directly. Rev. Gaffney has provided conversation models to help bridge the tremendous divide between our differing opinions of guns so that we can take positive action. We can no longer be silent; we have to engage this difficult topic with people we disagree with if we are to come up with solutions to prevent the next attack."
   —Vy T. Nguyen, Executive Director, Week of Compassion

"Donald Gaffney offers an insightful and faithful perspective on the issue of guns in America. Here is an exploration of gun violence that encourages honest conversation with self, neighbor, and God. Gaffney's book offers a way forward just as many religious Americans are beginning to recognize the social and theological costs of silence with regard to gun violence in all our communities."
   —Matthew Crebbin, Lead Pastor, Newtown (Connecticut)
   Congregational Church, UCC, and Clergy First
   Responder at Sandy Hook Elementary School

"A welcome entry into one of our most fraught national conversations. A gun owner, Gaffney looks respectfully at both 'gun rights' and 'gun control' perspectives. By including the troubling U.S. history of the myth of redemptive violence, the intersection of gun laws with race, and the complex biblical record of violence, Gaffney ensures that it will be no easy conversation. It is, however, an enlightening one, leading beyond talk to faithful action."
   —Sharon Watkins, Director, National Council
   of Churches Racial Justice Initiative

"Gaffney offers a timely resource for those longing to faithfully engage the enormous problem of gun violence in America. *Common Ground* rewards open minds with insightful examples and thought-provoking questions that seek to carve out a space in our 'us vs. them' cultural milieu where diverse voices are simultaneously welcomed and challenged."

> —William M. Shelburne, Presbyterian minister
> and co-organizer, Leaves of the Tree project, a
> response to gun violence in Savannah, Georgia

"Transparently speaking from his own social and cultural location as a white Christian clergyman who both owns firearms and is a committed activist in the movement to end gun violence, Gaffney invites readers to consider their own and America's troubled relationship with gun violence and culture. He offers helpful questions with historical, biblical, and cultural reflection to support readers as they listen deeply to their own stories and the experience of others. His journey will resonate with many who wish to work for a common solution to gun violence across the broad and increasingly polarized reaches of U.S. society from a place of faith, grief, repentance, and hope."

> —Laurie A. Kraus, Director, Disaster Assistance
> for the Presbyterian Church (U.S.A.)

COMMON GROUND

COMMON GROUND

Talking about Gun Violence in America

DONALD V. GAFFNEY

WESTMINSTER
JOHN KNOX PRESS
LOUISVILLE · KENTUCKY

© 2018 Donald V. Gaffney

First edition
Published by Westminster John Knox Press
Louisville, Kentucky

19 20 21 22 23 24 25 26 27 28—10 9 8 7 6 5 4 3 2 1

Unless otherwise indicated, Scripture quotations are from the New Revised Standard Version of the Bible, copyright © 1989 by the Division of Christian Education of the National Council of the Churches of Christ in the U.S.A., and are used by permission.

The Sandy Hook Promise in appendix A is reprinted by permission.

Book design by Drew Stevens
Cover design by Marc Whitaker/MTWdesign.net

Library of Congress Cataloging-in-Publication Data is on file at the Library of Congress, Washington, DC.

ISBN-13: 9780664264550

Most Westminster John Knox Press books are available at special quantity discounts when purchased in bulk by corporations, organizations, and special-interest groups. For more information, please e-mail SpecialSales@wjkbooks.com.

To those who feel under siege or caught in the cross fire from the postured rhetoric that has controlled the issue of gun violence for so long, *Pie Iesu Domine dona nobis pacem.*

Pius Lord Jesus, give them peace.

CONTENTS

Chapter 5
TALKING ABOUT GUNS AS CHRISTIANS

87

Chapter 6
BEYOND CONVERSATIONS

103

PREFACE

I grew up in the 1950s in a quaint New England town. I was a member of a nearly 250-year-old Congregational church—a traditional, white, wooden structure on Main Street. It was a life right out of Norman Rockwell's paintings. My father was a high school teacher there for over thirty-five years, and both my parents were civically active. When it was time for me to start grade school, the town had just completed a new structure, and I attended there from first through fourth grades.

Like many people, after college I moved away and for the most part put my hometown behind me. A confluence of several factors—my mother entering a local care facility for the last years of her life, my classmates and I all turning sixty years old and wanting to reconnect, and the growth of Facebook—renewed my affinity with my hometown. A sister-in-law and her family still live in town. My niece's husband works as a custodian for the school system.

The town is Newtown, Connecticut, and the school where I started first grade was Sandy Hook Elementary School. On Friday, December 14, 2012, a man with a Bushmaster semiautomatic rifle shot his way into that school and killed twenty first-graders and six faculty/staff members. None of my friends or family members was killed, but friends of friends were.

My niece's husband was not at Sandy Hook School at the time, but he was pressed into special service for the arrival of President Obama that weekend, and early the following week he had to go into the school building to help remove food from the kitchen.

The nation was shocked, and we—the Newtown community—were plunged into intense grief. I shared my grief with my local congregation in the midst of that Advent and Christmas season. At a retreat two months after the shooting, I was convicted that my silence in the face of this violence was an acceptance of the status quo and that by remaining silent I would be complicit in future violence.

I started searching the Web and reading. I followed the responses of fellow Newtowners. I tracked both gun control and gun rights organizations online. I became an early supporter of Sandy Hook Promise because I liked the fact that they simply wanted to honor the lives lost, were open to all possibilities, and encouraged having the hard conversations on all the issues. I learned some of the history of gun violence in this country and legislative attempts to curb it. I read summaries of Supreme Court decisions on the issue. And I started having conversations about guns and gun violence in response to the promise I'd made. I have made it a point to have a conversation, not a dialogue, debate, or argument.

I'm a Christian and an American. I've been an ordained minister within the Christian Church (Disciples of Christ) for over thirty years and a professional geologist with Michael Baker International, a major civil engineering company, for more than forty years. For the past several years I've had the privilege of sharing conversations about guns and gun violence in a wide variety of settings. Some people have known I am a minister, and some have not. I've talked with lifetime NRA members and staunch gun control advocates, and others across the spectrum between those extremes. Regardless of whether the other person has changed their mind or not, I have grown in knowledge and understanding of the various roles guns and gun violence have played in our individual and collective lives.

I have always approached these conversations prayerfully, aware that if I look and listen I will see and hear Christ present, regardless of any individual's claims early in our time together. Christ was a unique individual, and we too are each unique individuals. Within our uniqueness, we all are made in the image of God and are beloved of God. There's a popular saying many Christians claim: "In the essentials unity, in the non-essentials liberty, and in all things love." It's not intended as an excuse to avoid critical self-examination or lively conversation. It does remind us that thoughtful Christians are free to have opinions that are radically different than ours. Our challenge is to love through those differences, honoring each other in those differences as we each seek to follow a common God. This is especially critical in today's polarized atmosphere around the topics of guns and gun violence.

As you go through this book, my prayer is that you, too, will grow in knowledge and understanding of this deep and complex issue. You can choose to read and reflect on the topics in this book on your own, or you can organize a small group to talk about it together. Have a conversation: with yourself, with members of your congregation, or with others. At the start of your conversations, don't be surprised if others don't feel the same way about guns and gun violence as you. We each come with our own stories, and we grow by listening and sharing our stories with each other. Welcome all, regardless of how crazy you might secretly think their perspectives are.

Throughout the book, I will share my personal history. This is for illustrative purposes only. My story is my story, and the details are not exemplary. You are encouraged to develop and share yours. I will share as both a Christian and an American, and I encourage you to do so also. I mention various books and movies throughout the book, and more are listed in the back. These resources can offer additional perspectives and information on the issues at hand.

To help you get a sense of how wide open this issue is, think for a moment about your coworkers, members of your congregation, and others in your community. Do you know gun owners? If you know people with guns, are they hunters or recreational shooters? Do you know people who have a concealed-carry permit and routinely carry a handgun?

Does anyone you know wear a gun as part of their occupation? Are they in law enforcement, or do they work for a security firm? Do you know people who have served in the military or are serving now? Do you know anyone who collects guns? Have you ever seen anyone wearing an NRA baseball cap?

Do you see vehicles in local parking lots with decals, magnets, or bumper stickers indicating support for gun rights or gun control? Do you have friends who are vocal proponents of either of these groups? Are you uncomfortable when they start talking about guns or gun violence? You are not alone!

Let's explore guns and gun violence in America together. We can gain the confidence we need to speak what we each individually believe on this important and controversial issue.

ACKNOWLEDGMENTS

I started this manuscript on December 14, 2017, the fifth anniversary of the massacre at Sandy Hook Elementary School in Newtown, Connecticut. I completed the draft manuscript during Easter 2018. Between those dates, I struggled mightily.

Guns and gun violence were in the news more days than not during that time. There were mass shootings and public outcries. Some days I didn't think I could write fast enough. Other days, I just found myself sitting and waiting. As memes increased, I intentionally minimized my interactions on social media. Still, I was aware of the many shootings making national news as I was preparing this manuscript. I sensed the mood of the nation continuing to shift and was uncertain whether some of what I have written would be obsolete prior to publication. But I have written what I have written, and I trust the outcome to God.

I wish to thank my wife and my family as they have tolerated my responses to the Sandy Hook Massacre for more than five years now. The congregation and leaders at Central Christian Church of Hermitage, Pennsylvania, initially provided comfort and then support as I saw a need to address gun violence within my particular denomination, the Christian Church (Disciples of Christ). As a response grew, former and current Pennsylvania regional ministers and other regional leaders came alongside for more prayers and support. The National Benevolent Association sponsored a workshop on guns and gun violence that I facilitated at the Disciples' 2017 General Assembly.

When it came time to put these words down on paper, a Sandy Hook classmate providentially came back into my life. Bruce Baxter, thanks for coaching me through this process. My editor, Jessica Miller Kelley, helped immensely with both enthusiastic encouragement and practical advice. My therapist, Joe Peters, helped me wrestle with the Sandy Hook Massacre and its impact on my life. Finally, I owe a special debt of gratitude to Gonzalo Castillo-Cardenas, a professor at Pittsburgh Theological Seminary, who opened my eyes to many ways of seeing as we explored the sociology of religion together.

USING THIS BOOK IN A GROUP

This book can help individual readers reflect more deeply on the issue of gun violence in America and become more equipped to have important conversations about this issue as we seek solutions as a nation. However, those willing to undertake this reading as a group and start practicing these conversations in the context of a Sunday school class, small group, or specially convened discussion group can know they are taking a significant step toward breaking down the divisiveness that inhibits real change.

The leader of this discussion should be someone who knows the basics of group dynamics and can facilitate the conversation without monopolizing the group. The leader must be able to be firm with those who would monopolize, and gently draw out those tentative to engage. The leader needs to be attuned to the leading of the Spirit, as well as to the time limit set aside for the discussion. The leader should be sensitive and open to hearing various positions on guns and gun violence, because they are present within every group. I have never been in a group conversation about guns in which everyone was of one mind.

Wade into the water slowly. Trust in the power of prayer, and start with that. Start praying for the group before the first meeting, growing in confidence that God is in each person, regardless of their opinions. God is one, but God is represented in manifold and diverse ways. Even within the Trinity we see unity with diversity.

Always start and end with prayer. Focus on our unity in love for God and each other. Ask for the guidance of the Spirit, and acknowledge that Christ is the silent listener to every conversation. Ask for the openness of heart and mind that only God can give, so that we may come to see things in creative new ways, all to God's glory. Maybe it's my Irish heritage, but I feel best when I'm fully enveloped with God. A paraphrase of a brief part of the Breastplate Prayer of St. Patrick allows me to be wrapped and ready: *Christ before me, Christ beside me, Christ behind me, Christ to guide me.*

After prayer, there are simple, fairly standard rules for conversations about sensitive topics. A few Protestant denominations have guidance available on their websites. One side benefit of these conversations will be an increased knowledge of the resources of your denomination. There are several versions of conversation rules out there on the Web, and they can generally be boiled down to a few basics.

1. CONFIDENTIALITY

Confidentiality fosters a sense of security and trust within a group. It's hard enough to talk openly about how we feel about guns or gun violence without having to worry what might circle back to you through a friend of a friend of a friend. Unless explicit permission is given, don't share stories outside of the group. I will not repeat personal stories I've heard in confidence without permission, and I don't expect others to share mine, either. Your own stories, on the other hand, are your stories. Even though you may be hesitant at first about sharing them outside the group, eventually you may want to tell your stories. That is okay, as long as they are your stories.

2. TRUST

You have acknowledged God's presence and asked for God's guidance. Trust that it will be provided. Resist the temptation to steer the conversation in the direction you think it should go. This temptation to lead others to your understanding or position seems especially strong when talking about guns and gun violence. This is not a debate you can win by employing what you think is a rational argument. Let God do the leading, and trust that the conversation has power beyond the time limits of the group meeting.

There has to be an understanding among members of the group that no one will be pressured. We all are afraid of getting burned if we share too deeply. We've seen it. We've done it. It hurts. Everyone is responsible for himself or herself, and everyone is responsible to each other. If you start to get upset, it's okay to take a time-out. Conversations about guns can get really hot or tense very quickly if one person says something that really bothers you. It's okay to put some distance between yourself and the conversation. You can withdraw. Simply excuse yourself and leave the room for a few minutes. If you can catch yourself early enough, it will not seem like anything out of the ordinary to anyone else—just a visit to the restroom or to get a drink of water or a cup of coffee. I will not cajole you into staying engaged. That is abuse. We are not going to abuse each other; we are just going to have a conversation. Your simple action may help to defuse tensions building in other members of the group as well. You may find others deciding to take a break at the same time.

3. RESPECTFUL DIALOGUE

Pay close attention to the communication: listening and speaking. These are the fundamentals of good conversation. Listening is first and foremost. Listen to others before speaking, unless you are asked to share by the leader. Listen carefully and respectfully. Do not interrupt the speaker, but it may be appropriate to ask a clarifying question during a pause. You may also want to repeat what you thought you heard for confirmation that you did indeed hear the speaker properly.

If I'm having a good conversation, I consider what has been said before me. I want to respond to what I've heard, not react to it. If I respond, I reflect about how what I've heard affects me, about how I'm impacted by it. As I reflect, I recognize both feelings and thoughts welling up within me. I need to think past the thoughts to those feelings to see how my feelings drive my thoughts. I tend to be very rational, and I often divorce myself from my feelings. I may even have to admit they are "my" feelings so that I don't talk about them as separate from me. I need to own my feelings as much as my thoughts. We all have to acknowledge our own feelings and thoughts.

Being attentive while others are speaking and thoughtful in our own speaking is hard with a topic as volatile as guns. We have to work at releasing our preconceptions and relaxing our mood. When we finally do speak, we can speak from our own experience. It is so important that we each speak from our own core, our own feelings and thoughts. Anyone can parrot a meme they've heard a few times. Common knowledge and generalities are not the makings of good conversation. I especially don't like it when people attempt to tell me what I think or feel by couching generalities in "you" statements. Good conversation means sharing from the openness of our own hearts and our own minds. It does not mean attempting to manipulate another person into places they are not ready to go, or putting words in another's mouth.

If we honor and respect each other, if we trust God and each other, if we actively engage each other in reflective give-and-take, and if we open our hearts and minds, the conversation will be more than just good. It will be great!

Chapter 1
OWNING OUR STORIES ABOUT GUNS AND GUN VIOLENCE

Our views on social and political issues are not formed in a vacuum. The stories we bring to the table are essential to understanding our own perspectives and those of others. So we begin by reflecting on our childhood exposure to guns, experiences we've had in adulthood, and other influences that have shaped us.

GUNS IN OUR CHILDHOOD

Each one of us has a unique history with guns. I've already shared a little of my background, including that my father taught high school. For most of that time, until I was in middle school, he taught vocational agriculture. I grew up on a small farm that was his showcase and a proving ground for his students. We mostly grew table vegetables: sweet corn, tomatoes, squash, lettuce, cucumbers, beans, carrots, beets, and so forth. We also had a full orchard and other fruits: strawberries, raspberries, peaches, plums, cherries, pears, and apples. We sold fruits and vegetables from a picnic table under a maple tree at the end of our driveway.

I was the youngest of four sons, and we each also raised animals: heifers, sheep, goats, chickens, turkeys, and rabbits mostly. Often if townsfolk had an animal that had grown from a cute baby to an unmanageable monster, it would end up at our farm. All our animals were raised for sale or meat, except the farm dogs and barn cats, of course.

It seemed that everyone knew everyone back then. At least I had the distinct impression that everyone knew my family and me. Between my father's long tenure teaching and the sales at our truck farm, I didn't think I could ever get away with any troublemaking, and it seemed I was always too busy with farmwork to have the chance anyway. Looking back, I realize I had a very privileged early life.

Growing up in that environment, I can't remember the first time I shot a gun any better than I can remember the first time I hoed a row of corn, sawed a piece of lumber, mowed the lawn, or drove a tractor. When it was decided I was old enough, the tool was put in my hands and I was taught how to use it. Using it included knowing where it was kept so I could clean it and put it away when I was done. I learned how to fix and maintain the tools I was expected to use. And that applied to guns in our home.

The guns were kept in the main hall closet, leaning against the back wall. Shotguns were in the left corner, and long rifles were in the right. Most of the ammunition was kept on one end of the hat shelf above the coat rack in the closet, although some of the .22-caliber bullets were kept in an upper kitchen cabinet where they were more readily accessible. Throughout my time on the farm, a .22 rifle was my weapon of choice in the war to protect those vegetables and fruits from varmints: woodchucks, raccoons, squirrels, and birds of all sorts. I had a couple of different .22s to choose from, but I generally reached for a hefty Remington. The bolt action never seemed to eject the spent shells, but I liked the feel of the rifle so much I gladly put up with that nuisance. I inherited that favorite rifle, and I have it still today.

My brothers and I had lots of toy guns while we were growing up in the late 1940s and throughout the '50s. Most of the time we didn't bother with the caps for those guns that supposedly used them. I still have a futuristic paper-popping handgun; it looks like something right out of Flash Gordon. I used to have a toy flintlock pistol in my Davy Crockett days. We had military-style guns and rifles to use while rewinning World War II. We had Dick Tracy–style pistols to fight modern crime. And, of course, we had Western six-shooters for playing cowboys. I still have a Mattel "Fanner 50" handgun with part of its holster. Sometimes my guns were as simple as a pointed finger or a piece of bent wood broken from a tree. I won't say we played with guns all the time, but I will confess that we had a parakeet whose favorite phrase was "Stick 'em up! Stick 'em up! Stick 'em up!"

When we played, we recreated what we watched on television. We watched a lot of Westerns on our trusty black-and-white TV. TV studios seemed to crank out one series after another: *Wanted Dead or Alive, Cheyenne, Maverick, Sugarfoot, The Rifleman, Have Gun—Will Travel,* and similar shows were in strong demand. There were old Western movies and serials, and stars from those had their own TV shows, too: Hopalong Cassidy, Gene Autry, Roy Rogers, and others.

Consider how your childhood home and family environment shaped your awareness of guns. If you grew up on a farm, like me, chances are you were exposed to guns as necessary tools. Or perhaps one of your parents was in law enforcement or enjoyed hunting. Maybe your family had one or more guns for self-protection.

Think about how the era in which you grew up affected your experience of guns: Were movies more about gun-slinging cowboys or laser-shooting space weapons? If you grew up in the 1980s or '90s, conversations around guns may have centered more on the appropriateness of certain video games. Your parents may have objected to guns as playthings. All of these childhood influences are powerful in shaping our visceral response to the role of guns in our culture.

ADDRESSING GUNS AS ADULTS

As we reach adulthood, we are exposed to more harsh realities surrounding the use of guns and more complexity than we understood as children.

I came of age during the Vietnam War era. I went to college, but several of my friends went into the military. The government instituted a draft lottery while I was in college, and more of my friends enlisted. Friends joked that I won that lottery. My draft number was one, so it appeared inevitable that I would get drafted immediately after college. I went through most of the preinduction process, which started by my declaring whether or not I was a conscientious objector. My moral and religious background did not include a refusal to bear arms. I had been baptized and confirmed in the local Congregational church, but I also was a Connecticut Yankee farmer prepared to fight for what I held dear.

Even though I went away to college, during those summers back on the farm I dated a hometown girl. We were married in that white Congregational church on Newtown's Main Street after I completed four years of college and before I returned for a fifth and final year at Rensselaer Polytechnic Institute (RPI). The military draft ended before I graduated, so I wasn't called to serve.

After college, my wife and I moved from Newtown to western Pennsylvania. The move introduced us to another culture. Coal mines and steel mills were still in operation. Social stratification was determined by ethnicity, from the Scottish owners and Irish managers to the Eastern European mill hands and miners. Pennsylvania has a well organized fish and game commission, and within the commonwealth there are many large land tracts set aside for hunting and fishing. Most rural families with roots in Pennsylvania hunt or fish. Many of these traditions are based in the desire to put meat on the family table in spite of low wages received in the mills and mines. Now they are expressed in the tradition of Deer Day. The first Monday after Thanksgiving is the first official day in Pennsylvania for deer hunting using a rifle. Many rural schools are closed on this day to allow young people to hunt with their parents. For a young person, shooting their first deer is a true rite of passage. On Deer Day, the woods are full of hunters, and shots can be heard coming from many wooded areas. I am not a hunter, but we live in the country and have enough woods on our property that others usually hunt there. Often they share the meat when they are successful.

My wife and I have been blessed with two sons. Having children often prompts serious conversations about guns. My wife and I had several such discussions when our boys were young. I first became aware that she had a very different background with guns during those discussions. I wanted to give our sons toy guns, but my wife was opposed to the idea. As I pressed her for reasons, she began to share stories from her own childhood.

During her early childhood, she had lived in the city of Bridgeport, Connecticut. She and her family would occasionally hear the sound of gunshots coming from the streets outside their house. Her father felt the need to have a gun in the house to protect his family. He was a first-generation Italian American. He had experienced prejudice during World War II and responded by enlisting in the army during the Korean War. My wife's father used to wave a pistol around at home while saying to his children, "I brought you into the world, and I can take you out of it." He'd learned that from his father, who was a butcher by trade and would say the same thing while wielding a meat cleaver. With perceived threats both inside and outside the home, my wife was terrified of guns.

As you might imagine, guns became one of those issues that had to be worked out in our marriage. The Christmas after our older son turned three years old, I wanted to give him a Western outfit, complete with a pistol. My wife would have nothing to do with it. I didn't see what the problem was. From my perspective, it was perfectly normal. I bought the outfit, and he received it that Christmas. My wife saw this as a classic example of my failure to hear her side of the story. I asserted my right as the father of a son. At first, she asked me to consider how much our son liked play-acting what he saw on TV, and how his having a toy gun could make him more violent. I protested that I had played with all sorts of toy guns and that I thought I turned out okay. It was only after she opened up to me about her own history and her own fear of guns that I took her seriously. I respected and appreciated her honesty. I also had to admit that giving our son a gun was something I wanted to do, not something he wanted.

We settled on allowing our boys to have only anachronistic or fantasy guns. I was able to give them toy guns representing the old Wild West or those similar to the ones used in Star Wars movies. I kept my guns out of sight. My rifle was broken down, with the bolt separated from the barrel and stored under lock and key. My toy guns are in a storage bin.

OUR EXPOSURE TO GUN VIOLENCE

My earliest memory of gun violence was Ernest Hemingway's suicide in 1961. I read about it in magazines of the time, but we didn't discuss it in my family. I still have vivid memories of the assassination of John F. Kennedy, the shooting of Lee Harvey Oswald, and JFK's funeral. I remember the assassinations of Martin Luther King and Robert Kennedy in 1968 and the aftershocks those deaths caused. Watching network news, special reports, and nightly broadcasts on our black-and-white TV during that violent summer of 1968 made a lasting impression.

Until a few years ago, other than my wife's issues, I never gave guns or gun violence much thought. Then an esteemed colleague and mentor committed a murder-suicide. His wife had terminal cancer, and he apparently couldn't bear it. One morning, he shot her in her sleep, called the police to report it, and then shot himself. A year before the Sandy Hook Massacre, one of our older son's best friends from high school committed suicide. He had been battling depression most of his life. The weekend after Thanksgiving he parked his car on a bridge and turned a shotgun on himself.

For some people, witnessing gun violence—whether through the news or the experiences of family and friends—makes them want to limit the availability of guns. For others, seeing such violence in the world makes them see guns as a necessary means of protection.

SUZANNA GRATIA HUPP'S STORY

Suzanna Gratia Hupp was born in Arizona and from a very young age loved to play with toy guns.[1] She and her older brother would role-play Westerns, cops and robbers, and army with a collection of toy guns. When her brother was ten, he was given a Red Ryder BB gun by his parents. Both she and her brother learned safe handling of firearms using that BB gun. By the time she was nine, her family had moved to Texas. Soon after moving, she was watching some boys who were shooting a pellet gun. As one boy passed it to another, the second boy put his finger on the trigger, causing it to shoot a pellet that hit Suzanna in the right arm. The pellet lodged fairly deep, so the wound was cleaned, stitched, and bandaged. After several weeks, the pellet had migrated to just under the skin, so a second simple procedure removed it. It was Suzanna's first experience as a gun victim. The incident and its aftermath impressed upon Suzanna the importance of vigilant gun safety. She'd learned to respect all guns and handle them safely, but she now realized that not everyone had learned those lessons. She needed to be on guard when people around her were armed.

During her college years in Arizona, Suzanna was introduced to shooting real firearms at inanimate targets, and she enjoyed the sport. She soon bought her own handgun for sport and self-defense. Returning to Texas after college, she soon acquired another handgun, even though it was illegal at that time to carry a handgun, open or concealed, in Texas. However, she knew she was a "good guy" and justified breaking the law on occasion. Then, in social conversation, she discussed her dilemma with someone in law enforcement. He urged her to carry her weapon every day and to take other precautions to avoid being a victim.

That advice reinforced her commitment to be vigilant in all phases of self-protection. She routinely did all the rituals the officer had suggested to her when approaching her car or her front door. She assessed the conditions and verified that no one was hiding or lurking where they shouldn't be. She typically had her hand on her firearm in her pocket while doing the assessment.

She got to use her firearm once to save her sister's cat, by shooting a rattlesnake that had frozen the cat in place. Both Suzanna and her brother-in-law heard and understood where the snake was at the same time. She grabbed her pistol and ran to get within close range, while her brother-in-law went inside to get his shotgun. His shotgun was locked in a rifle safe, and the shells were locked in a separate cabinet. While he was inside, she shot the snake dead with her pistol. She is convinced the cat and not the snake would have been killed if they had to wait for him to unlock the safe and gather up the shotgun and shells.

On October 16, 1991, she joined her parents for lunch at a buffet-style chain restaurant in Killeen, Texas, called Luby's. She was friends with the manager on duty that day, so he joined them. It was "Boss's Day," so the place was busier than usual. As she sat down in the crowded cafeteria, she made a mental note of several other friends and acquaintances nearby. After their main meal, they got coffee and dessert. Her friend the manager was called to help deal with an issue in the kitchen.

Suddenly a pickup truck smashed through the front window and stopped about fifteen feet from their table. At first Suzanna thought it was an accident. Then she heard gunshots and thought it was a robbery. Her father flipped over their table to act as a shield, and the three of them— Suzanna, her father, and her mother—hid behind it. The gunshots continued, and when Suzanna peeked around the table she was surprised to see the driver simply shooting one person after another.

She thought she could grab her purse and get her gun, but then she remembered deciding that the time she would need it would be when she was in her car late at night, not in a crowded restaurant at lunchtime. So instead of the gun being in her purse, it was in the parking lot in her car.

Her father decided he had to do something, so he lunged at the attacker. The attacker simply turned and shot him with one of his two guns. That action got the shooter to change the direction of his walk through the restaurant. Meanwhile, in the smoking section, someone had managed to shatter a back window. People were pouring out through the broken window to escape the scene. Suzanna decided to take a chance, urged her mother to come with her, and then ran through the window herself. Once outside, she was reunited briefly with her friend the manager in charge, who directed her to a safe place across the street. After a few minutes, she started to come back toward the restaurant and recognized a local policeman. As soon as the "all clear" was given, they approached the restaurant together. Through the manager, Suzanna learned that both of her parents were dead. Later, she learned that a total of twenty-three people had been killed.

Suzanna was angry that the law did not allow her to carry her firearm into the restaurant. She had the opportunity to take a clear shot and has said in many interviews since that she could have ended the shooting much earlier if she had had the gun with her. Soon after, she decided to advocate for the right to carry concealed firearms. She testified before the Texas legislature and saw a concealed-carry law go into effect in January 1996. She then became a state representative herself. Suzanna Gratia Hupp continues to fight for Second Amendment rights.

GABRIELLE GIFFORDS'S STORY

Gabrielle "Gabby" Giffords was also born and raised in Arizona.[2] Gabby was exposed to a variety of cultures and life circumstances early, which led to her decision to work in public service, especially in the areas of education, health care, environment, and immigration reforms. She entered politics in 2000 as a member of the Arizona state legislature. Arizona has very liberal gun laws, and while serving there she supported gun rights. She had a personal handgun, a Glock 9mm.

When Gabby decided to run for the U.S. Congress in 2006, gun rights were not high on her agenda, and she favored keeping guns out of the hands of those who are mentally ill or convicted felons. Consequently, the National Rifle Association (NRA) gave her a "C" rating and nominally supported her opponents. Nonetheless, Gabby was elected by her progun constituency and was serving in the capital when, in 2008, the Supreme Court struck down and Congress repealed the handgun ban imposed on people in Washington, DC. At the time, she stated that the law was contrary to a long tradition of gun ownership in the United States. Her legislative district included not only Tucson but also Tombstone, and she learned not to be surprised at seeing constituents carrying firearms.

Gabby ran for reelection twice and won both times. Whenever she returned from Washington to Arizona, she made a point to go out and meet her constituents. Typically, she held simple "meet and greet" events at which she did not make speeches but had conversations about issues of interest so that she could be informed when she returned to DC. Gabby called these events "Congress on Your Corner."

Her third campaign, in the fall of 2010, was the toughest and closest, but she won reelection again. Immediately after the first week of the new session of Congress, she returned to Arizona to hold a "Congress on Your Corner" event outside a Safeway store in a suburb northwest of Tucson. The event was organized by her district director and her local community outreach director. It was scheduled to start at 10 a.m. on Saturday, January 8, 2011. That morning, staff members and friends arrived a little early, as did Gabby. They set up tables and a banner. John Roll, Arizona's chief federal judge, was one of the friends who came out to wish Gabby well. Other people who wanted to thank her, encourage her, and just meet her started to form a line. They signed in and waited their turn.

Shortly after the event began, a young man approached the table and said he wanted to meet Gabby. He was told to sign in and wait his turn. He went to the back of the line, but at about 10:10 he rushed back to the table. He pulled out a 9mm Glock pistol with a thirty-three-round magazine and shot Gabby in the head at point-blank range. He then turned and shot her district director, her community outreach director, and the federal judge. He turned again and started shooting his way down the line of people. He went through the thirty-three rounds in less than a minute.

The shooter also had two fifteen-round magazines with him, but he fumbled when he tried to reload. Several people rushed him, some pinning him to the ground while others grabbed the magazines and the gun. A man with a legally concealed pistol in his pocket came running from a nearby store, saw the man holding the shooter's gun, and told him to put the gun down. Fortunately, both the man with the legal pistol and the man who had disarmed the shooter acted and reacted calmly. If the legal gun owner had shot first to disarm the man holding the gun, without telling him to put it down and waiting for a response, the mass murder could have ended with the accidental shooting of someone who helped stop the violence.

The shooter had a history of mental illness, did not trust the government, and specifically wanted to assassinate Gabby Giffords. At the end of the shooting spree, five people were declared dead at the scene, a sixth—a nine-year-old girl—was declared dead at the hospital, and thirteen were wounded.

Gabby managed to survive but was in a coma for a week. In less than two weeks, she could stand with assistance. In a month, she could speak a little. The bullet, however, had paralyzed much of her right side. She had to struggle to walk, her right arm was completely paralyzed, and her right peripheral vision was gone. She learned to write left-handed using an iPad. She had weekly speech-therapy sessions.

Her husband, former astronaut Mark Kelly, became her spokesman. They worked together on what to say and where to invest their time and energy. Initially, Gabby went back to the floor of Congress, but within a year she decided to step down.

They thought about how she had represented Tombstone in Congress. The most famous gun battle there, at the O.K. Corral in 1881, was about gun rights and gun control. Back then, Tombstone had an ordinance that people had to surrender their guns when they arrived in town. Officially, the Earps were acting to enforce that ordinance, which the Clantons chose to ignore. When Gabby was shot, anyone over eighteen in Arizona could carry a loaded weapon openly, and anyone twenty-one or older could carry concealed weapons. Even people with a criminal record and mentally ill people could not be denied that right. It seemed to Gabby and her husband that common sense had been abandoned.

They talked about gun violence and what they might do to make a difference. The massacre in Newtown on December 14, 2012, drove them to action. They reached out to their support network to see if funding could be available through donations. It was. Next came the name. While serving in Congress, Gabby was always a moderate, trying to be reasonable and responsible. As Mark later wrote, "We knew what the name should *not* contain: no *guns*, no *rifles*, no *control*, no *violence*. We weren't *against* anything; we simply wanted to bring people together to solve real problems."[3] They named the organization Americans for Responsible Solutions and publically launched it on the second anniversary of the Tucson shooting.

REFLECTION AND CONVERSATION

Suzanna Gratia Hupp and Gabrielle Giffords were both born and raised in the southwestern United States. They both survived mass shootings, and both were spurred to respond. Each chose her own path. While the paths are different, each is true to her personal history before the shooting.

Using the questions below, reflect on your own personal history with guns and gun violence. If you are reading in a group, consider setting a timer for each person to share their personal history (questions 1 through 3), then continue to discussion of subsequent questions.

1. What was your exposure to guns while growing up, both real guns and toy guns, and in the media you consumed?

2. How did your thoughts about guns change as you became an adult, got married, or had children? Do you own any guns now? What types?

3. What do you remember about gun violence in your past? What is the first violent gun death you remember hearing or reading about? Have you ever witnessed or been directly affected by gun violence? Was it an accident, a suicide, a murder, or a shooting during war?

4. Why do you think Suzanna Gratia Hupp and Gabrielle Giffords came to such different conclusions about placing limits on the right of citizens to own and carry firearms? What are some factors that might have played a part in shaping their positions?

5. Do your opinions lean closer to Hupp's, Giffords's, or somewhere in between? Why? Can you understand how people can come to different conclusions? Can you articulate in a nonjudgmental way the opinion of those with whom you disagree?

Chapter 2

AMERICA'S CULTURE OF GUNS

Listening to a gun owner talk about his or her gun is a good starting point for considering guns in popular culture. Today, guns have become so much more than tools for hunting and weapons for resolving conflicts. New technologies allow gun owners to easily create their own variations of some guns. In addition, guns have become collectible. Very few gun owners have only one. I've watched YouTube videos telling me what firearms I need to have for different purposes, including personal protection, hunting, and sport shooting. Some walk the viewer through several "must have" firearms for the home, or showcase fine collectible specimens.

The language of guns has become our language. Once this was brought to my attention, it became painfully obvious how much I speak in terms of guns and violence. Try making a list of gun references as you think of them or hear them.[1] There may be too many to catch, but give it your best shot. Once you have a pen and paper handy, you'll be ready to pull the trigger. You will be blown away by how quickly your list grows. As you get better and better at spotting gun language in your sights, you can load your own conversation with references to guns. Fire away! But I'd suggest you scope out your target audience for this first so that it doesn't backfire and someone goes ballistic.

UNIQUELY AMERICAN

It's clear that gun culture is strong in the United States. The British Broadcasting Corporation (BBC) has published online articles critically examining our gun culture. I trust the BBC to generate relatively unbiased gun statistics gleaned from a wide variety of sources. Following the mass shooting in Parkland, Florida, they ran an article entitled "America's Gun Culture in 10 Charts."[2] The following information comes from that article.

The United States has roughly 270 million guns, or approximately 90 for every 100 residents. (I have seen U.S. sources that claim we now exceed one gun for each man, woman, and child.) While this number is conservative, the next nine highest-rated countries are significantly lower. Yemen has 55 guns per 100 people, Switzerland about 46 guns per 100 people, and Finland about 45 guns per 100 people; all three countries have compulsory military service for all men over eighteen. The remaining six of the top ten gun-owning nations all have between 30 and 35 guns per 100 residents.

In the United States, guns are involved in 64 percent of all homicides. This compares with 30.5 percent, 13 percent, and 4.5 percent in Canada, Australia, and England-Wales, respectively.

Mass shootings account for only a very small proportion of all gun deaths. For example, in 2014, of 33,594 firearms-related deaths, 21,386 were suicides, 11,008 were homicides (of which only 14 were in mass shootings), and 1,200 were other gun deaths, including from accidents and war. Military assault-style weapons have been used in some mass shootings, but more than half of our firearms murders involve handguns.

The weapons found in the hotel room of the Las Vegas Massacre shooter ranged from $200 handguns to military-style rifles costing $1,500 or more each. The twenty-three weapons in that room plus the nineteen other weapons found in the shooter's home, along with all of their accessories, were estimated to have cost more than $70,000.

The events and circumstances of our history have created a culture that still influences us today and with which we have to grapple when working together to solve the problem of gun violence. The BBC has attempted to understand our culture in another article: "Why Are Americans So Obsessed with Guns?"[3] They find it baffling that we continue our love affair with guns even at the cost of so many American lives. The article states, "With the constitution in one hand and a rifle in the other, pioneers claimed the Wild West, and a new kind of citizenship was born." Guns are our foundation and identity, a symbol of our freedom, in ways they are not for most other nations.

The United Kingdom changed its gun laws after a school massacre in Dunblane, Scotland, in which sixteen children were murdered in 1996. Besides laws, however, the main difference is the place of guns in everyday life. The United Kingdom has gun lovers involved in shooting sports, but the idea of gun use in self-defense is "generally pretty shocking in Britain, even within the shooting community." Britons entrust such use of guns to the police and armed forces. On the other hand, for many of us it seems to make sense to arm ourselves when we feel threatened, and we seem to all feel threatened now. The BBC cites three other main factors driving our gun culture: the ready availability of guns (without standard background checks or other measures), the gun business (a $13.5-billion-a-year industry, with the NRA as its lobbying agent), and social and cultural pressures (we are evenly split on key gun issues, and the divide fuels both sides).

REVOLUTIONARY BEGINNINGS

Before we go further, I need to clarify a couple of points. First, I use the term "American" when discussing the history of the United States of America for brevity's sake, despite the fact that Native Americans populated the continent for millennia before Europeans arrived and the continents of North and South America are also American. Also, I have chosen to capitalize Native American, Black, White, and terms for other groups consistently when referring to race or ethnicity.

America's history with guns started when Europeans first landed in North America and came as settlers to what they called the New World. Some of my ancestors settled in New England when that area was still a British colony. The white Congregational church building on Main Street in Newtown (now a community meeting house) has a gold-leaf rooster atop its tall steeple. Since colonial times, people have claimed to have taken shots at that rooster. There are rumors that it has holes in its side from musket balls.

America was considered wilderness, and people had to be ready to protect themselves. Guns were the ideal choice. Although primitive by today's standards, those guns provided a sense of security in a new environment and served as a valuable tool for securing meat for food. Colonists almost immediately discovered that the American wilderness was populated by native people. As Europeans claimed land in America for themselves, conflict with those natives was inevitable, and guns gave a decided advantage to the colonists in those conflicts.

As time went on, European militaries had a presence in the American colonies to protect those colonies from other colonizing powers. The British armies also sought to maintain order across their colonies as the seeds of revolution began to grow. One way they attempted to do this was to control access to firearms and ammunition in the colonies. England stopped exporting these to the colonies, except as army provisions. England then sought to disarm the colonists through search and seizure of guns and powder found outside their homes. The colonists had for some time organized themselves into militias to fight natives. Those militias relied on ordinary men and privately owned guns, along with commonly held guns and powder stockpiled for emergencies. British armies seized stockpiles whenever they could. The first shots of our Revolutionary War were fired in defense of a stockpile of firearms and powder in Massachusetts.

That history helps to explain why the right to bear arms was essential to the nation's founders.

FRONTIERS AND VIOLENCE

Americans have always had a frontier. In the very early days, the frontier was only a few days' journey on foot from the Atlantic coast. At our back was the ocean, and beyond that was Mother England. Before us was the raw, untamed wilderness where each individual had to be alert to dangers at every turn. Both natural dangers and "savage" natives

were a constant threat. As we pushed westward, that frontier went before us. Behind us was civilization with its social
and political rules and structures. First it was England, then
it became the major cities back east: New York, Philadelphia, and Washington, DC.

Americans lived in the tension between what lies
behind and what lies ahead: we lived on the frontier. Such
an American "was one who had defeated and freed himself from both the savage of the western wilderness and the
metropolitan regime of authoritarian politics and class privilege."[4] The importance of this concept is generally traced
back to a talk given by Frederick Jackson Turner in 1893,
entitled "The Significance of the Frontier in American History." It was reinforced by Theodore Roosevelt's multivol-
ume history *The Winning of the West*, written in the first
years of the twentieth century. In 1920, Turner expanded
his talk into a full volume.

Our intrusion into the frontier set up a violent conflict whereby we were reborn, regenerated, or redeemed,
and the savage other was killed, exterminated, or assigned
to the hell of subjugation. The dynamics of this American
experience were reflected in the Leatherstocking novels
of James Fenimore Cooper, who used the racial tension
between Whites and Native Americans as the context for
exploring other fundamental tensions, such as social roles,
class structures, and gender purity.[5]

America's violent history is not unique, of course,
and we could name genocides and other acts of mass
violence that have occurred throughout history and
around the globe. In his book *Gunfighter Nation*, Richard Slotkin explains that what makes our violence dis-
tinctly American "is not necessarily the amount or kind

of violence that characterizes our history, but the mythic significance we have assigned to the kinds of violence we have actually experienced, the forms of symbolic violence we imagine or invent, and the political uses to which we put that symbolism."[6]

During the physical expansion of America across the continent, Slotkin says, our economy was generally prosperous as we took advantage of "free" land and slave labor. Violence was the way Europeans managed to keep both Native Americans and enslaved Africans in check. Guns were important tools enforcing superiority. In the late nineteenth century when the western frontier appeared to close, America moved from a long period of economic prosperity to the worst depression in its history, coinciding with the social upheaval that accompanied the transition from primarily an agrarian society to primarily an industrial society. This linked the loss of frontier with hard times, cemented the idea of the frontier with success, and allowed folk legends to become cultural icons.

Davy Crockett and Daniel Boone are real American legends, with their personas growing over time to mythic proportions. Both were frontiersmen, both were skilled marksmen, both fought in war, and both of their life stories have been conflated. They actually lived about a generation apart. Today there is a sporting group called the Boone and Crockett Club. It was formed in 1887 to promote wildlife management and ethical hunting, with Theodore Roosevelt as one of its founders. Its name is a tribute to Boone and Crockett as archetypes of the hunter-frontiersman. The club's formation coincided with public outcries over the wholesale slaughter of the American bison and the growing interest in preserving wilderness areas. Today it promotes itself as a conservation club and is best known for its scoring system and record keeping of trophy-worthy big game.

THE PROMISED LAND, MANIFEST DESTINY, AND THE IDEA OF REDEMPTIVE VIOLENCE

Religious components also fueled the use of violence to tame the frontier. As Europeans started settling this land, they had a sense that the land was special and that they were special for living here. They saw themselves as exceptional people in an exceptional place. As they read their Bibles, they saw themselves as a new Israel moving into a new promised land. The more they spread out (displacing the natives), the more that sense grew. This new promised land seemed to be limitless in its capacity to offer Europeans opportunities. It appeared that God had given them this land. They just needed to keep themselves in God's favor. By the middle of the 1800s, people spoke of "Manifest Destiny": Americans' destiny to claim the land from sea to shining sea, conquering or converting the peoples already living there. They mimicked the Israelite conquest of their promised land as recorded in the Bible.

Merriam-Webster's Collegiate Dictionary defines manifest destiny broadly as "an ostensibly benevolent or necessary policy of imperialistic expansion." This definition underscores the idea that Manifest Destiny really was an American policy. While our ancestors saw it at the time as a benevolent gift of the gracious God, we have come to see that it really was propaganda to provide a rationale for our violence toward American Natives as our nation expanded its borders.

We have always found a rationale to fight. From the Declaration of Independence to the attack on the Twin Towers, we believe we are right and our foe should be vanquished. Over that time we have gone from claims of war as a last resort to war as a first response, and we even consider preemptive strikes. Our growth as a nation has been tied to our willingness to go into the frontier, confront and conquer the savages, and spread civilization as we know it.

We have gone from a group of colonies fighting oppression to a superpower attempting to police the world. We stand for life, liberty, and the pursuit of happiness! Since the Declaration, we have put our actions within a religious context and placed "a firm reliance on the protection of divine Providence." That context includes more than just a "God is on our side" mentality. We have identified a need to take extreme, violent actions to secure our life and liberty, and to save us from those who would deny us our understanding of those freedoms. When we have acted with violence to save ourselves, and others, most of the time we have been successful. We have then seen that success as God's blessing on our actions. Put in religious terms, our salvation has been realized through redemptive violence.[7] Our country and those who stand for freedom have been saved time and time again by our violent actions.

This concept of redemptive violence is critical to our understanding of violence and its application to gun violence. It asserts that we can save others and ourselves only insofar as we are willing to violently oppose those who don't agree with us. It is a short jump from what we do as a nation to what we do as individuals. We see this redemptive violence promoted again and again in our folklore and our popular culture, but it has rarely been more visible than in the era of the two world wars, when good and evil seemed to clash on a global stage.

GOOD GUYS WITH GUNS

Consider the story of Alvin York, born in 1887 in Tennessee. In his mid-twenties, he was "born again," became a regular churchgoer, and tried to live according to the teachings of the Bible. During World War I, the United States instituted a draft program to bolster its armed forces, and York initially registered as a conscientious objector on the grounds of his faith. He struggled with violence in the Bible and the morality of war. After being given time to reflect on it, he decided that he should "render unto Caesar what is Caesar's" and do his full duty as a soldier.[8] He was sent to France to serve in the infantry as a private. He soon was promoted to corporal. Then in 1918, he and sixteen others were sent across the German line to silence a machine gun position that was keeping the Americans pinned down. Before getting to the position, they came under fire from Germans. Six Americans were killed and three were wounded, but they got the Germans to surrender and found themselves with prisoners. After that initial skirmish, York found himself the highest-ranking American soldier and so took charge. He left his men guarding the prisoners while he went ahead toward the machine guns. He methodically worked his way, picking off Germans as he went. His ability and good fortune frustrated the commander of the local German forces to the extent that he offered to surrender. York readily accepted. York and his remaining ten men returned to their unit's post with over 130 German prisoners and many weapons. He was promoted to sergeant, received the Medal of Honor for his efforts, and was hailed as an American hero. In many ways he personified the rugged, plain-spoken frontiersman who demonstrated strong faith combined with patriotism.

He ultimately—and reluctantly—allowed a movie to be made about his life and experience. Released in 1941, *Sergeant York* was the highest-grossing film that year, garnering eleven Academy Award nominations and winning two, including for Gary Cooper as best actor for his portrayal of Sergeant York. The movie provided a timely boost for America's involvement in World War II by not only celebrating a war hero but assuring viewers that allegiance to God was compatible with violence in response to the threat of outside evil powers.

Media is often a reflection of the culture's concerns and needs. It's no coincidence that Superman was created in the 1930s to save Americans from the evil predators, mobs, and gangsters prevalent during the Great Depression. Captain America is in turn modeled after Superman. He and other superheroes were introduced in the late 1930s and early '40s as the nation looked for redemption from the evils of fascism and Nazi Germany.[9]

During the relatively stable years following World War II, the familiar genre of the classic Western became a way to process and reinforce methods of dealing with the problem of outside evil. Americans needed a savior, a deliverer—a good guy with a gun. They needed a man (they were all men back then) with a special skill (usually with a weapon) and self-control in the face of evil who could save the day. Such a man would often appear mysteriously, as a stranger. He would dispatch evil by defeating the villain in a showdown or in some other dramatic violent fashion. Peace and stability would return, and the hero would ride off into the sunset.

To me, the movie *Shane* is the prototypical Western. *Shane* is a 1953 film that won an Academy Award for color cinematography and was nominated for five others, including best picture. The title character wanders into a frontier town to discover local farmers are being driven out by a ruthless rancher. Shane is hired to help one good farmer work his homestead. Shane avoids initial attempts to fight the rancher and his men. Ultimately, however, Shane takes that farmer's place in a shootout, killing the evil rancher and his black-hatted hired gun. This apparently was not Shane's first gunfight. After having saved the farmer, his family, and the town, Shane rides off into the sunset. While the basic story is simple, many themes are explored within the movie, including frontier family life, the role and purpose of guns, and how to deal with the problem of evil.

We only need to think of the Lone Ranger, Batman, and Superman to see this basic formula of good people being saved from evil by a violent deliverer again and again. It has been said that "the elemental outline of the Western is more familiar to us than our own biography."[10] As I think about my own understanding of Westerns on TV and in movies, I find this to be true in my life.

This classic Western setting has a particular foundation: "Behind the gun is the man; behind the man is a woman. She gives the whole enterprise merit and purpose."[11] The "whole enterprise" is a stable, family-centric community, with peace, prosperity, and domestic tranquility. Society is raised to a new level of civility and respectability. This is the redemption gained through the Western hero's violence. The community is "reborn" through the violence.

With the development of the Cold War, the Western formula morphed into spy movies and TV shows with invincible good guys dispatching evil through violence. The series of James Bond movies is the most recognizable, but there were others, including the TV series *I Spy* and *The Man from U.N.C.L.E.* (Even though James Bond was British, he was franchised by the American movie industry.) This classic genre—and with it, the notion of redemptive violence—has rightfully been challenged and critiqued in various ways through "anti-Westerns." The major players within the Western—the community, the white-hatted hero, and the black-hatted villain—are distorted in anti-Westerns, showing that good and evil are not as clear-cut as we so often like to believe. Sometimes this distortion has the community itself as the source of evil. Sometimes the hero dies, bringing judgment instead of salvation onto the community. Several themes are stressed in these anti-Westerns, including the end of the Wild West, a more complex relationship between Native Americans and White Americans, heroes who are alienated professionals rather than wilderness men, and non-Western settings for exploration of Western themes—particularly urban and futuristic settings.[12] Anti-Westerns can be as varied as *Blazing Saddles* and *The Godfather*. John G. Cawelti has suggested that "the old epic of the American frontier as the myth of White America's conquest of a savage wilderness is in the process of giving way to a new mythical dialectic of multiculturalism which cannot be contained within the patterns of the Western."[13] However, it seems we keep coming back to variations of this genre for safe exploration of conflicts and moral fantasy, as in the recent TV series *Hell on Wheels* and *Westworld*.

GUNS AND RACE

Questioning the whitewashed myths of morally pure folk heroes was nothing new for America's racial minorities. Those "heroes" were part of a narrative celebrating the civilized White man subduing the non-White "savage." Black Americans always knew the dark side of that narrative. Before the Civil War, Whites used guns to quell slave uprisings. In his book *Gun Fight,* Adam Winkler recounts the largest of those, which occurred in the territory of Louisiana in 1811. A group of slaves took guns and swords from their plantations and marched toward the city of New Orleans, setting fire to residences and gathering more slaves and weapons along the way. They grew to number in the hundreds and formed militarylike companies. In response, the governor called out the militia and distributed to it weapons from a local arsenal. Within two days, the revolt was squashed, with about one hundred slaves killed in the process.[14] Guns were strictly for Whites. Slaves were banned from owning them.

In his book *Negroes and the Gun*, Nicholas Johnson notes that there were always ways for Blacks to obtain firearms. With the passage of the 1850 Fugitive Slave Law, Blacks gathered in armed communities for mutual protection. For many Blacks, resistance to slavery was the equivalent of war. Black abolitionists were willing to meet Whites not with prayer, kind words, or smiles, but "as they meet us—prepared for the worst."[15] In the time leading up to the Civil War, Blacks became more emboldened as they understood that the country and its laws were for Whites but that the fundamental human rights for which the Revolutionary War had been fought were also their rights. Those rights included self-defense, using arms if necessary. Blacks—freemen, fugitives, and slaves alike—understood their marginal and largely unsympathetic status and took steps for self-preservation independent of any U.S. laws of that time.

Many slaves fought for the Union cause during the Civil War and kept their weapons upon returning to the South. But Whites attempted to maintain supremacy by continuing to ban Blacks from owning weapons and confiscating them whenever they were found. White patrols emerged to disarm and terrorize Blacks. The most well-known of these was the Ku Klux Klan. Even though the U.S. Army occupied much of the South, it was largely ineffective against these White patrols. In response, Blacks began to organize informal, armed militias of their own. This led to many skirmishes and battles between the Black and White militias throughout the South, as well as an estimated five thousand Black lynchings in the thirty years after the Civil War.[16]

Various state and local laws throughout the South severely constrained Black lives, including restrictions to work, travel, and property rights. These typically included a prohibition on Blacks owning firearms. However, Blacks argued that they were now citizens and as such had the right to bear arms. In 1866 Congress discussed and passed what ultimately became the fourteenth amendment to the Constitution in 1868. This established the legitimate basis for Black civil rights, including the right to bear arms. This fueled fear among southern Whites that Blacks could be elected to rule in counties where they had a majority of citizens. Whites typically were "better organized, better armed, and potentially more desperate"[17] and often succeeded in disarming and intimidating local Blacks. As reported in numerous Black newspapers of the late 1800s and early 1900s, there was a general mistrust of government support of Black civil rights. Blacks were encouraged to arm themselves and to carry firearms whether or not it was legal. Anecdotal evidence suggests that many, if not most, Blacks were armed for both self-defense and mutual protection within Black communities.

Looking to the civil rights movement roughly one hundred years later, Blacks were increasingly frustrated with ineffective peaceful protests, and police abuse was often tied to Klan violence. Self-defense seemed the only viable option. Malcolm X preached that since the government was unresponsive, Blacks needed to protect their lives and property "by whatever means necessary."[18]

Fearful as Whites were of an armed Black population, Adam Winkler goes so far as to say that "if it hadn't been for the Black Panthers, a militant group of Marxist Black nationalists committed to 'Black Power,' there might never have been a modern gun rights movement."[19] Black Panthers in Oakland, California, openly carried guns in public, where everyone, including police, could see. Huey Newton, one of the Panthers, had attended law school classes and discovered that open carry was allowed in California as long as it was "non-threatening," that is, the weapon was not aimed at anyone. After an armed standoff with local police, the Black Panthers began to change the relationship between Blacks in the community and the Oakland police. In response to the show of force by the Black Panthers, the California State Legislature passed a law banning public carrying of loaded guns. It was signed into law by conservative governor Ronald Reagan. As the Black Panthers went national, the FBI under J. Edgar Hoover considered them a criminal element to be eliminated.[20] Open carry, it seemed, was also only for Whites.

We still see this double standard today as Black men and boys are shot and killed by police and wary Whites. In March 2018, for example, Sacramento police mistook Stephon Clark's cell phone for a gun and shot him to death in his grandmother's backyard.[21] John Crawford, a twenty-two-year-old Black man, was shot and killed in a Walmart while carrying a BB/pellet rifle for sale in the store.[22] Many other instances of deadly force being used against unarmed Black men have made headlines.

These double standards are fueled by false stereotypes, which exacerbate gun violence and make conversations about the solution more complicated. Not every Black person carrying a gun down the street is a criminal. Not every White person carrying a gun in public is a responsible gun owner looking to save the day.

SEPARATING FACT FROM FICTION

Today we recognize Westerns as fictionalized and romanticized accounts of history, but we still struggle with the glorification of modern violence. In the nightly TV coverage of the Vietnam War, journalists were given freedom to report on the war as they saw it. Back home we saw not only the battles won but also the battles lost. We saw the good, the bad, and the ugly. We saw the dead from both sides of the conflict. We saw the cost of the war, and public support for it was lost. John Wayne made the movie *The Green Berets* to promote the war, but many young people saw it as outright propaganda. I certainly did. Later movies such as *The Deer Hunter* (considered a post-Western) and *Apocalypse Now* provided a more critical perspective.

Though we should have learned by now that things are more complicated than the classic Westerns depict, we seem to have reverted to a pre-Vietnam view of "good guys" and "bad guys." When the Twin Towers were brought down by terrorists on September 11, 2001, that action was used as a rallying cry for patriotism. Once more America was called to redemptive violence. We needed to save ourselves and the rest of the free world, and so we declared a "war on terror." And this time, as we sent young people off to fight our battles, the journalists were embedded with the troops, and their reports had to be cleared by the military prior to release. Gone was coverage of platoons lost and planeloads of American dead returning. The war was sanitized for our protection. The reality that "war is hell" has been lost to the general public as the enterprise continues to be glorified as a pure and noble cause.

We have new folk heroes such as Chris Kyle, a U.S. Navy SEAL who served four tours of duty during the Iraq War as a sniper. He was born in 1974 in Texas and was raised in a devout Christian family. His father was a deacon, and his mother taught Sunday school.[23] He was given his first hunting rifle at age eight. He joined the Navy SEAL program in 1999. During his time in Iraq, Chris Kyle's skill with rifles became legendary. He routinely trained with a variety of rifles so he could choose the best one for any given situation. He had over 150 confirmed "kills" as a sniper, and he claimed that his longest successful shot was over a distance of more than a mile. He became known as the deadliest sniper in U.S. military history. During his four tours, he was shot twice and survived detonations of several improvised explosive devices. At the time of his discharge in 2009 he had accumulated over a dozen awards and decorations, including a Silver Star and four Bronze Stars with Valor.

After his discharge, Chris Kyle ran a tactical training business and worked with fellow veterans. Several books were being published about Navy SEALs and their operations at that time, and he wrote an autobiography titled *American Sniper* that was published in 2012. On February 2, 2013, he and a friend, Chad Littlefield, took a third veteran, Eddie Ray Roth, to a target range to do some pistol shooting. Once there, Roth shot and killed both Kyle and Littlefield before they had even unholstered their weapons. Roth used pistols supplied by Kyle, and was later found guilty of the murders. Roth suffers from posttraumatic stress disorder (PTSD) and was given a life sentence without parole instead of the death penalty. In 2014, Clint Eastwood directed a movie, *American Sniper*, loosely based on Chris Kyle's autobiography. That movie was nominated for six Academy Awards.

Kyle's story highlights several factors pertinent to the current state of America's gun culture. Not only was Chris Kyle an extremely talented marksman, making him a model for gun enthusiasts honing their own skills, but he used his expertise in service of his country and thanked God every night that he had survived another military operation.[24] His untimely death at the hands of a fellow soldier suffering from PTSD raises concerns about mental health and gun ownership, as well as the question of whether having armed bystanders—even those trained at the highest level—is an effective way to stop a shooting.

REFLECTION AND CONVERSATION

Guns and violence in our history, folklore, media, and current events all shape the way we respond to the problem of gun violence in America today. Think about how your personal history from chapter 1 fits within our greater American history. Consider the following questions or discuss them with your group.

1. Have you read the Declaration of Independence or the Bill of Rights lately? If not, find a copy and read it. Can you get a sense of why the colonists revolted? How does reading the Second Amendment in the context of the Bill of Rights affect your understanding of its place as a law of the land? Can you see dangers in routinely considering it out of context?

2. What images come to mind when you think about America's gun culture? Are they mostly historical or contemporary? Do you think this culture is essential to what it means to be an American?

3. How do racial minorities fit into your image of gun culture? How do you see racial stereotypes played out around gun violence? How do these stereotypes affect your beliefs on whether guns should be carried openly in public?

4. Do you believe violence can be redemptive? That is, are there occasions when people are "saved" through violence? Do you think that violence that saves or benefits us (whether individually or as a community/ nation) is approved by God?

5. Where do you see a distinction between "good guys" and "bad guys" today? Is this distinction justified or a result of unnecessary division in our society?

Chapter 3

GUNS AND GUN VIOLENCE IN AMERICA

You may be reading this book because you are troubled by gun violence and mass shootings making headlines so frequently in our nation. From a group of children in an Amish schoolhouse to open-air concertgoers in Las Vegas, no community is immune to the threat of gun violence. Now that we've explored our personal and common histories, let us examine this presenting issue.

FROM NEWTOWN TO NOW

Soon after the massacre in Sandy Hook, I felt two things: (1) the entire nation was mourning with us, and (2) what happened there could have happened anywhere in America. Newtown, Connecticut, was inundated, first with media and then with cards and gifts of all shapes and sizes. Thousands upon thousands of stuffed animals and toys arrived. Warehouse space was needed to receive, organize, and distribute them. Items were forwarded to organizations and individuals who might be able to benefit from them. Monetary gifts were received, and nonprofit organizations were established with nationwide reach. It seemed people all across America didn't know how to respond but felt they had to do something.

We found ourselves to be members of a club no one wants to join: the gun violence survivors club. We heard from Columbine survivors and others across the nation who had lived through this before us. It has happened so many times that the pathway to recovery is known, but that recovery doesn't have a timeline.

At the same time, those of us who thought we knew Newtown so well had a hard time fathoming how it could happen there. The massacre destroyed our quaint New England nostalgia and replaced it with a dark sense of foreboding. Nothing and nowhere is off-limits to gun violence anymore. That was a lesson we learned.

In the years since the massacre at Sandy Hook Elementary School, many more place names have been added to the litany of massacres. Schools continue to be targets: Marshall County, Kentucky; Parkland, Florida; and Santa Fe, Texas, made national news, while other shootings have not. The response to Parkland, where seventeen people were killed and another seventeen wounded, was similar to that of Newtown. After Newtown, the parents of the young victims spoke out. After Parkland, the families of the victims were joined by survivors from the high school, who could speak for themselves. That dark foreboding continues to be a reality. Mass shootings have happened and will continue to happen. Schools won't be the only target. Nothing is off-limits, from a nightclub in Orlando, Florida, to a Waffle House in suburban Nashville, to anywhere people gather. Other cities, towns, and communities will join the gun violence survivors club.

When I started talking with Pennsylvanians about gun violence, they brought up Nickel Mines, an Amish community in Lancaster County, Pennsylvania, where in 2006 a gunman went into a small school and killed five girls before killing himself. It was notable not only as a school shooting but also because of the response of the Amish. They practiced forgiveness. This shooting inspired PBS to create "The Amish" as part of its *American Experience* series. It also fueled the creation of the film *The Power of Forgiveness*, winner of best documentary at the 2007 Sun Valley Spiritual Film Festival.

Before Newtown, the most infamous school shooting was in 1999 at a high school in Columbine, Colorado, where a pair of gunmen killed thirteen people before committing suicide. But there were well over one hundred school shootings in the decade leading up to Columbine, and in the time since Newtown there has been nearly one school shooting a week, somewhere in America. The vast majority of our states have been affected.[1]

GUNS AND SHOOTINGS

Conversations about gun violence are sometimes impeded by disagreements over terminology, particularly when people who don't own guns exhibit lack of knowledge about the weapons they are discussing. As used here, *gun* is a common name for a firearm, that is, a device that uses an explosive charge to launch a projectile. In some legal contexts, firearms can be understood as limited to small, portable pistols, revolvers, and shotguns or rifles with barrels less than a designated length, such that they can be carried easily in a concealed manner. At other times, firearms may include everything from pistols to military-style rifles that carry bullets in high-capacity magazines and can shoot as fast as someone can repeatedly pull the trigger.

A *shooting* is when shots are fired from a gun. Death or injury do not have to result from the shooting, so while this term includes gun homicides and suicides, the use of this single term to define different levels of activity—from simple shots fired, to a person wounded, to a person killed—can lead to misunderstandings and challenges of validity.

Similarly, *mass shooting* is used when many people are killed. There is no set number, but since the FBI identifies four or more murders within a short time and distance by a single perpetrator as a mass murder, that rule is generally applied to shootings. While this is a subjective term, I use the term *massacre* to describe the mass shooting at Sandy Hook because it was a slaughter of innocent children. It can also be applied to an extremely large and indiscriminant shooting, such as the 2017 Las Vegas Massacre, in which the perpetrator used modified semiautomatic weapons to spray open-air concertgoers with bullets.

Answering the question "How much gun violence is happening today?" is not simple. In 2005, a document entitled *Firearms and Violence: A Critical Review*, published by the National Academy of Sciences (NAS) through its National Research Council (NRC), pointed out that there is a "relative absence of credible data central to addressing even the most basic questions about firearms and violence."[2] On the other hand, there is a wealth of descriptive information about "the prevalence of firearm-related injuries and deaths, about firearms markets, and about the relationships between rates of gun ownership and violence."[3] However, the committee found that the available data often doesn't support unambiguous conclusions. The creation of the National Violent Death Reporting System (NVDRS) at the Centers for Disease Control and Prevention (CDC) was an encouraging step in better data collection. However, the NAS-NRC report recommends caution when interpreting data.

The CDC itself states that about 56,000 violent deaths occur in the United States each year, more than two-thirds of them suicides. About 32,000 people die from gun violence each year, 19,000 by suicide and 11,000 by homicide. The remaining 2,000 firearms deaths are mostly the result of accidents, legal interventions, or unknown causes. The numbers fluctuate somewhat from year to year, but they allow us to imply that over half of the violent deaths in the United States, including suicides and homicides, are from firearms.

Reviewing the data from 2003 through 2015, the death rate from firearms varies from roughly 8.5 to 10.5 per 100,000, and the overall average is just over 10 per 100,000. The death rate does not show a consistent trend from each year to the next, but when I looked at these years in three equal four-year blocks I saw that the average rate increased over time from 9.8 to 9.9 to 10.4 deaths per 100,000. Researchers using other CDC data going back to 1968 have shown that the death rate per 100,000 from firearms has increased over time.[4]

Sorting by race and ethnicity, the rate for American Indians/Alaskan Natives was essentially equal to the total average (just over 10 per 100,000). Whites were just under the total average (roughly 9.5 per 100,000). Blacks were just over one and a half times the total average (roughly 15.5 per 100,000). Asians/Pacific Islanders were less than one-quarter of this (less than 2.5 per 100,000), and Hispanics were about half the total average rate (about 5 per 100,000).

We need to be very careful how we interpret this data. It does indicate that Blacks have the highest rate of firearms deaths, while Asians/Pacific Islanders have the lowest. It is tempting to speculate why these differences exist, but it is doubtful that enough relevant data exist to warrant any inference.

DATA AND MASS SHOOTINGS

One noticeable effect of studying data is the loss of a sense of humanity. Each statistic involves many people—people who died from gun violence. A quick reread of the previous section would indicate how easily people can be replaced by numbers, as pollsters, government officials, and statisticians like to do. We sometimes feed this desire for numbers as we struggle to understand what all this gun violence means. However, we are so much more than just numbers. We all are individuals with names, faces, and personalities. We love and are beloved. We have families and friends. Each and every violent gun death is a trauma that numbers do not begin to touch.

Nowhere is this more obvious than with mass shootings. Mass shootings only account for a small proportion of all gun deaths. However, the trauma they inflict is far greater than what is indicated by numbers and statistics. And their impact will only get worse in the future.

Mass shootings are happening more frequently and becoming more deadly. This was the conclusion the BBC reached as it posted a list of the ten worst mass shootings since 1991, the year of the Luby's shooting in Killeen, Texas, where 23 people were killed. Five of those ten have occurred within the last five years: Parkland, Florida (2018, 17 dead); Las Vegas (2017, 58 dead); Sutherland Springs, Texas (2017, 26 dead); Orlando, Florida (2016, 49 dead); and San Bernardino, California (2015, 14 dead).[5] That's 164 people in five communities! Eight of those ten worst mass shootings have occurred since 2006, adding Sandy Hook, Connecticut (2012, 27 dead); Fort Hood, Texas (2009, 13 dead); and Blacksburg, Virginia (2007, 32 dead) to the list. The tenth shooting on that list is Columbine, Colorado (1999, 13 dead). There is no way data and statistics can do justice to the people who died and the communities who have suffered so greatly.

There were other deadly mass shootings before 1991, of course. At the University of Texas in 1966, a former Marine wheeled an arsenal of weapons onto an elevator and went to the observation deck of the Clock Tower in the heart of the campus. For more than ninety minutes he shot at passersby, killing sixteen people before he himself was shot. Back then, it really was an anomaly. Blame was placed on the shooter's apparent mental illness, and we didn't think we had to do anything more than mourn the dead. Fifty years later, we know better. We are struck with a foreboding sense that another mass shooting can and will happen again at any place and any time here in the good old U.S.A. We can't keep living like this. So what can we do?

In its "America's Gun Culture in Ten Charts" article, the BBC cites Gallup polls that indicate that a significant majority of U.S. citizens oppose a ban on handguns but that 46 percent are dissatisfied with our government's laws and policies and would like to see them made stricter. Another 39 percent are satisfied with our laws, while 8 percent are dissatisfied and would like to see laws less strict. A direct check of the Gallup data indicate that there was a shift after Parkland, not reported by BBC, such that the most recent numbers here are 67 percent in favor of stricter laws and policies, 28 percent satisfied, and 4 percent wanting less-strict laws.[6]

MAJOR GROUPS ADDRESSING GUNS TODAY

The major groups debating and advocating for different solutions to gun violence fall into two main camps, which I will call "gun rights" and "gun control." Gun rights groups sometimes are referred to as "the gun lobby" or "Second Amendment rights groups." These groups include the National Rifle Association (NRA), with its political action committee the Institute for Legislative Action (ILA); the National Sport Shooters Federation (NSSF); and the Second Amendment Foundation, with its Citizens Committee for the Right to Keep and Bear Arms. The most visible spokesperson for these groups is Wayne LaPierre of the NRA. LaPierre has held various leadership positions in the NRA over the years and currently has the title of executive vice president and CEO. The gun rights groups publish reports and promote the research performed by the Crime Prevention Research Center (CPRC), an organization headed by John R. Lott, author of the book *More Guns, Less Crime*. The methodology used by Lott in his book has been challenged as ambiguous and inconclusive, but it is still often cited.

Gun control groups sometimes prefer to call themselves "gun violence prevention groups." These groups include Giffords, with its Giffords PAC and Giffords Law Center; the Coalition to Stop Gun Violence (CSGV), with its Educational Fund to Stop Gun Violence (EFSGV); and Everytown for Gun Safety (Everytown). Giffords is the merger of two previous groups, Americans for Responsible Solutions and the Legal Community against Violence, with Gabrielle "Gabby" Giffords and Mike Kelly as its chief spokespeople. The CSGV is a group of roughly four-dozen organizations with the shared goal stated in the coalition's name. Everytown for Gun Safety previously was Mayors against Illegal Guns and is connected with the grassroots advocacy group Moms Demand Action for Gun Sense in America. Michael Bloomberg is Everytown's most well-known member. Everytown produces reports and fact sheets for use by others. In addition, the Violence Policy Center (VPC) is a gun control group that analyzes and interprets available data on firearms and violence and publishes its findings. The VPC is often the source for facts and figures used by gun control advocates, even though its findings are also often questioned.

There are many other organizations on both sides, and most are readily accessible through the Web. One should be wary of data provided by advocacy groups, however, as both sides tend to repeat the information they have generated and discount information generated by the other side. The websites for both the gun rights' CPRC and the gun control's VPC show selective use and manipulation of data in ways that favor their stated positions. Whenever I want to find data concerning guns and gun violence, I try to go to a government or third-party source (such as CDC or BBC) or find the data and its interpretation from at least two different sources. Then I have some assurance of the validity of the data and its interpretation. I do not simply take the first number I find.

It can be useful to know and seek to understand the positions of the major groups addressing guns and gun violence in America. I think we can carefully pick our way through what we find published by both sides, so we can "eat the meat and throw the bones away." Sometimes it can be as simple as terms used, for example, what we call firearms. The CSGV calls them weapons. The NRA says to call them guns, firearms, pistols, rifles, shotguns, whatever they are, just not to call them weapons because weapons carry a negative connotation.

Gun Rights Groups

The NRA considers itself a defender of freedom in a "war against the Second Amendment." It actively lobbies elected officials through its NRA-ILA to promote legislation that strengthens the individual right to bear arms. It considers legislation that would limit in any way firearms, ammunition, or firearm accessories to be detrimental to that right. It sees its mission as protecting freedom (as set forth in the Second Amendment) over against providing safety at the expense of that freedom. It has been instrumental in the passage of several federal laws, including the 1986 Firearms Owners Protection Act and the Protection of Lawful Commerce in Arms Act of 2005. The NRA financially supported Donald Trump's presidential campaign and has reaped the benefits of that support with regulation changes and appointments of gun rights supporters to positions of power.

The NRA continues to fight to reduce and modify firearms regulations, to relieve firearms owners from what it sees as federal abuse and harassment through excessive paperwork, exorbitant taxation, and illegal search and seizure of personal property. It has proposed its own approach to school safety with a program called National School Shield that combines security infrastructure, technology, armed personnel, training, education, and policy. The NRA runs an extensive media and publications network to promote its agenda.

Gun Control Groups

On the other side, the CSGV is not a single organization, but it reflects a trend within the gun control movement to combine forces and form alliances and coalitions to strengthen their position against the NRA and other gun rights organizations. Gun control groups want freedom from gun violence. For example, the CSGV agenda includes requiring universal background checks for all firearms transfers, including online and private sales. It would prohibit the manufacture, transport, and possession of "assault weapons" and their high-capacity cartridge magazines. It opposes armed insurrectionists and armed White supremacists, who intimidate the public through openly carrying weapons. The CSGV opposes policies that would allow guns in schools and other public spaces, and opposes "stand your ground" laws that protect those who use gun violence as an early option in resolving conflict. It opposes the gun industry's immunity from civil suits and protection against civil recourse on behalf of gun violence victims.

The CSGV supports innovative policies, like use of a gun violence restraining order (also called an extreme risk protection order), to protect domestic partners from gun violence. It supports expanding this type of protective restraint beyond the bounds of traditional marriage to include all types of intimate relationships and close what it calls the "boyfriend loophole" in domestic violence restraining orders. It looks to the day when guns are required to microstamp their unique identification numbers onto ammo cartridges, to facilitate tracking of guns used in crimes. These are examples of innovative policies the coalition pursues that can be data-driven and technology-based.

The CSGV works for policies that are based on behavioral risk rather than mental health diagnosis. Federal law currently prohibits people determined to be "mentally defective" (a subjective term that some define as those who have assigned representatives to handle at least some of their affairs) or who have been involuntarily committed to a mental institution from owning firearms. Rather than rely on a legal definition or mental health diagnosis, the CSGV seeks to remove access to firearms when people are in a personal crisis. It cites data that indicate mental illness is not a significant risk factor for violence against others but that firearms are a highly successful means of completing suicide. It therefore wants to limit firearms access to at-risk individuals during times of crisis. The CSGV relies on public awareness to move toward changes in public policy. While its sister organization the Educational Fund to Stop Gun Violence does research and publishes reports, officers and members of the CSGV routinely publish in media that are generally aligned with this group but are not typically associated with it explicitly.

MAKING THEIR CASE

Recently, I received letters in the mail from both the NRA and the Giffords political action committee (PAC) within two weeks of each other. Here are brief summaries of both.

The NRA letter is addressed "Dear Fellow American" and was sent to urge me to stand with other gun owners "to defend our country and our freedoms." (Full disclosure: I am not a current or previous member of the NRA.) It continues: "You and I know our enemies are not going away. They have more resolve than ever. And they'd rather tear our nation apart at the seams than give up on their extreme leftist agenda." The letter claims there are 100 million gun owners in America that benefit from the NRA's efforts, and that it is a nonpartisan, grassroots organization with millions of patriotic Americans as members (just under six million, according to its website, so using the NRA's numbers, that equates to 6 percent of all gun owners in America). The letter promises to do "whatever it takes" to defend our freedoms. After a review of membership options, costs, and benefits, the letter concludes, "Now is the time to STAND and FIGHT with NRA." It is signed by Wayne LaPierre.

The Giffords letter is addressed to me personally. (Full disclosure: I have donated to Giffords in the past.) It is written in a personal tone and signed by Mark Kelly. It is a reflection on the events after the February 2018 shooting at Stoneman Douglas High School in Parkland, Florida, including the March to Save Our Lives in Washington, D.C. Kelly writes that student survivors of that shooting "converged on Washington, DC—and inspired people in over 800 cities across the United States and around the world—to demand that our leaders take action to stop our nation's epidemic of gun violence." He ties the fact that only one student killed in Parkland "had lived to see an 18th birthday" with Gabby Gifford's "only" birthday wish: "electing a Congress that will pass safer gun laws." The letter is a request for a contribution to support the Giffords PAC so that it can work to change Congress. "Elected officials are starting to understand that there is more to fear from us, united, than from the gun lobby and all their money and influence." Giffords's goal is to leverage the voices that have cried out "by the power of our votes."

These letters give us glimpses into those organizations that we might not otherwise have: the points they emphasize, the language they use both for those on their "side" and those on the other, and the emotions they are trying to elicit from the recipients of the letter. When I read them, I tried to appreciate their perspectives, view them critically, and not get swept up in their emotionalism. The bottom line was that both letters were looking for financial support. One way I can make a difference is through such support of a group or groups who have the same goals that I do. There are many groups out there, and I want to invest wisely.

THE CONSTITUTION AND THE COURTS

Regardless of the ways different groups make their case, passion and public opinion alone do not change laws. Many legal cases have been made dissecting the nuances of laws related to the possession of firearms. The second amendment to the Constitution, one of ten amendments that make up the Bill of Rights, is the primary amendment concerning guns: "A well regulated militia, being necessary to the security of a free state, the right of the people to keep and bear arms, shall not be infringed." However, it must be taken in context of the Bill of Rights' other nine amendments. The Fourteenth Amendment figures prominently in these debates as well.

We all have "certain unalienable Rights, that among those are Life, Liberty and the pursuit of Happiness." Originally stated in the Declaration of Independence, these rights were enumerated in the Bill of Rights and reinforced as "life, liberty, or property" in the due process clause of the Fourteenth Amendment. This amendment was passed after the Civil War, primarily to clarify that all former slaves were full citizens of the United States and of the individual states in which they resided. The individual rights of all citizens could not be denied without due process of law, and the rights of citizens of individual states could no longer conflict with federal law.

Part of the background of due process and the Fourteenth Amendment relates to state militias after the Civil War. All-White militias in former Confederate states attempted to strip Blacks of their weapons, often firearms earned by service in the U.S. military (the Union Army). With the passage of the amendment, not only was this practice of disarming Blacks clearly illegal, but as citizens Blacks were expected to serve in militias themselves and to be treated as legitimate military personnel.

It seems that from its inception, legal scholars have argued over the interpretation of the Second Amendment. Much of that discussion has centered on the first, prefatory clause: "A well regulated militia, being necessary to the security of a free state . . ." As late as 1939, in the case of *United States v. Miller*, the Supreme Court cited this clause in its decision. The National Firearms Act of 1934 was being challenged. That act called for the registration and taxation of so-called gangster guns: sawed-off shotguns, machine guns, and guns with silencers. Miller was arrested for carrying an unregistered sawed-off shotgun across state lines, and the appeal that his Second Amendment right was infringed went to the Supreme Court. As part of its ruling, the court stated, "In the absence of any evidence tending to show that possession or use of a 'shotgun having a barrel of less than eighteen inches in length' at this time has some reasonable relationship to the preservation or efficiency of a well-regulated militia, we cannot say that the Second Amendment guarantees the right to keep and bear such an instrument." It stated that weapons used by militias were firearms of the kind in common use, owned and kept by ordinary citizens, and the weapon in question did not meet that test.

Then, in 2008, the Supreme Court ruled on a handgun ban in effect in Washington, D.C. The case was

District of Columbia v. Heller, commonly referred to as "*Heller*." District of Columbia law at the time not only effectively banned handguns but also required any licensed firearms to be kept in a nonfunctional condition in the home. The court squarely addressed interpretation of the Second Amendment and determined that the right to keep and bear arms was an individual right, not restricted to use within or for militias. Individuals have a right to keep and bear arms for their own personal self-defense as well as for community defense. Since the most common firearm that citizens use for defense in their home is a handgun, the court ruled that Heller was within his rights to keep a handgun and to keep it in a functional condition in his home. There were registration and licensing components to the D.C. law, but Heller agreed to them as a condition of ownership during oral testimony, so the court did not rule on those requirements.

Shortly after this decision, it was tested in the case of *McDonald v. City of Chicago*. At that time, Chicago had laws effectively banning handgun possession by almost all private citizens. In 2010, the Supreme Court solidified the *Heller* ruling by declaring the laws in question unconstitutional. As part of its ruling, the court clarified that the right of individuals to keep and bear arms is one of the rights guaranteed by the Fourteenth Amendment.

These recent decisions have practical implications as we have conversations about guns in America. Some gun-control advocates continue to argue that the Second Amendment right only should apply to militias and to guns of the types used when we used to have militias. Neither of these claims were part of the *Miller* decision. That decision ruled that a sawed-off shotgun was not the sort of weapon that common, everyday people (ordinary citizens) would typically use if they participated in a militia. Therefore, it was not covered under the Second Amendment. (We now have the National Guard, and the evolution from militias to the Guard is yet another sidebar to the conversation about guns.) Some gun-rights advocates continue to point to Chicago's high crime rate "in spite of effectively having banned handguns there," but since those laws were overturned in 2010 with the *McDonald* decision, current crime in Chicago is not reflective of an area where a handgun ban is in place. Nonetheless, that city is still singled out. These are examples of false or misleading points made by advocates on both sides, when they repeat statements they have heard from others on their own side without checking the facts first. As we talk together, it is important that we speak from a point of knowledge rather than simply repeating what we have heard others say. It is better to take a few minutes, check things out, and tell the whole story than to repeat half-truths.

FEDERAL LEGISLATION

Just as court decisions have not leaned consistently one way or the other, federal legislation concerning guns in the past century has led to both gun control and gun rights groups claiming victories at various times. Following are some of the more famous federal laws.

Legislation promoting gun control typically has followed particularly egregious gun violence. In 1929, the St. Valentine's Day Massacre occurred when one Chicago gang lined up and gunned down seven associates of a rival gang. In response to this and other acts of Prohibition-era organized crime, the 1934 National Firearms Act required registration and taxation of uncommon firearms such as machine guns. It gave the government a tool to arrest gangsters for failure to register their guns. With passage of the law, the government did not have to wait until the guns became murder weapons to confiscate them.

Two acts passed in 1968, the Gun Control Act and the Omnibus Crime Control and Safe Streets Act, were responses to the assassinations of Robert Kennedy and Martin Luther King and the riots that followed. These laws prohibited the sale of handguns to minors; prohibited the sale of firearms to convicted felons, drug users, and the mentally ill; required serial numbers on firearms; established Federal Firearms Licensed dealers; and set licensing and record-keeping requirements for those dealers.

In January 1989, a gunman with a semiautomatic AK-47 rifle opened fire on a playground at the Cleveland Elementary School in Stockton, California. He killed five children and wounded over thirty others. In response, the Gun-Free School Zones Act of 1990 was passed, making it illegal for unauthorized individuals to have weapons within 1,000 feet of school property. The law was quickly challenged, and the Supreme Court ruled that Congress had overstepped its powers. In 1995 Congress passed what was essentially the same law, only this time it required prosecutors to prove that the firearm involved had moved in interstate or foreign commerce, making it less a gun violence prevention law and more a commerce law.

The Brady Handgun Violence Protection Act of 1993 initiated what ultimately became known as the NICS (National Instant Criminal Background Check System) for firearms. It was named in honor of James Brady, who was one of four people wounded during a 1981 assassination attempt on President Reagan. Brady's injuries left him permanently disabled, and he became a gun control advocate.

In 1994, the Violent Crime Control and Law Enforcement Act imposed a federal ban on assault weapons and large capacity magazines. Nineteen specific weapons, including the AR-15 and AK-47, were named in the act. This law was a response to what had become preferred weapons among the violent drug gangs of that era and was part of the government actions to get tough on drugs. The act passed with a "sunset" provision that it would expire unless it was reratified in ten years. Gun rights groups celebrated the expiration of this act in 2004.

Gun rights groups were largely responsible for passage of the Firearms Owners Protection Act of 1986, which rewrote and relaxed parts of the 1968 Gun Control Act. The Bureau of Alcohol, Tobacco, and Firearms (ATF, which added "and Explosives" to its name in 2003) was accused of abusing its powers under the 1968 act and harassing gun dealers. To protect against onerous government actions, the ATF was limited to inspecting dealers only once annually unless that inspection found multiple violations. This law also forbids the federal government from creating a national registry of gun owners.

The Protection of Lawful Commerce in Arms Act of 2005 was promoted by gun rights groups to protect firearms manufacturers and dealers against negligent liability for violence and crimes committed using their products. It is intended to protect them from lawsuits similar to those brought against the tobacco and automobile industries.

Gun laws are still mostly at the state and local level, but there is more clarity of the federal position from the recent Supreme Court rulings. We may or may not agree with those decisions, but they are the law of the land. And since the Second Amendment is tied to the Fourteenth Amendment, state laws must not violate the federal law, as interpreted by the court. Significant change to federal law would require another constitutional amendment.

Before we move to state and local law, there is one other Supreme Court ruling pertinent to the conversation: *McLaughlin v. United States*. In 1984, McLaughlin attempted to rob a bank and in the process "displayed a dark handgun and ordered everyone in the bank to put his hands up and not to move." McLaughlin and his accomplices were caught by police as they left the bank. The gun was not loaded. McLaughlin pleaded guilty to robbery but claimed he was innocent of the charge of assault by the use of a dangerous weapon because the gun wasn't loaded. In 1986 the court ruled against McLaughlin, stating three reasons: "First, a gun is an article that is typically and characteristically dangerous; the use for which it is manufactured and sold is a dangerous one, and the law reasonably may presume that such an article is always dangerous even though it may not be armed at a particular time or place. In addition, the display of a gun instills fear in the average citizen; as a consequence, it creates an immediate danger that a violent response will ensue. Finally, a gun can cause harm when used as a bludgeon." In a footnote to this decision, the Congressional Record was cited to indicate that "Congress regarded incitement of fear as sufficient to characterize an apparently dangerous article (such as a wooden gun) as 'dangerous' within the meaning of the statute."

STATE GUN LAWS

Each state has its own gun laws, developed since colonial times over "common law" history and codified to various levels. Restrictions on licensing, sales, ownership, open and concealed carry, and justified use vary widely across the United States. For example, Pennsylvania presently has concealed-carry reciprocity with Texas (meaning my Pennsylvania-issued concealed-carry permit would be valid if I were to vacation in Texas) but not with my home state of Connecticut. Connecticut is much stricter when it comes to firearms and licensing. Each state is different. This is why it is important to know state law as a basis for conversations around law and changes in law. This is part of what makes gun policy reforms so difficult.

Pennsylvania has attempted to balance individual rights and the good of the commonwealth in its laws, starting from a strong gun-rights position. Back when the Second Amendment was being proposed and discussed, Pennsylvania was a strong advocate for even less restrictive language than ended up in the amendment. Much of Pennsylvania was still frontier, and guns were needed for more than a militia. To this day, the Constitution of the Commonwealth of Pennsylvania includes this line: "The right of the citizens to bear arms in defense of themselves and the State shall not be questioned." Pennsylvania reads this as an individual right. Pennsylvania is a "presumptive" state— that is, the state presumes that any citizen openly carrying a gun has a legal right to it. That presumption can be challenged as soon as a citizen carries a gun in a concealed manner. There are subtleties to the regulations defining open and concealed carry. Any Pennsylvania citizen who carries a concealed firearm must have a license.

To obtain a concealed-carry license in Pennsylvania, one completes a simple, one-page form stating there is no legal reason why he or she should not be allowed to carry a gun and providing names, addresses, and phone numbers of two character references. Legal reasons for denying a license include felony convictions and an active Protection from Abuse (PFA) warrant in place against the applicant. In the event a PFA is issued, the gun owner must forfeit his license for the duration, and move his firearms outside of his direct control. The act of obtaining a license is very simple. A clerk for the county sheriff accepts the form, a positive photo identification, and twenty dollars; performs an electronic background check; photographs the individual; and prints out a laminated license good for five years. The entire process takes about five minutes. I know. I have a Pennsylvania License to Carry Firearms. It allows me to both open-carry and concealed-carry guns, and it is considered cheap insurance against potentially being arrested for concealed-carry of a weapon.

To be eligible to receive a License to Carry Firearms in Pennsylvania, no prior training is required and no specific firearms are required to be identified. However, since 1993 the Pennsylvania Legislative Reference Bureau periodically has assembled and published an unofficial summary of *Pennsylvania Laws Relating to Firearms*. Members of the Pennsylvania General Assembly make this 150-page book available for distribution. Some local legislators distribute it in conjunction with public meetings to discuss concealed-carry and other gun laws of general public interest.

I attended one such meeting led by the local county sheriff and county attorney. The sheriff is responsible for issuance of licenses and enforcement of the laws, and the attorney is responsible for prosecution of the laws and other legal issues such as misrepresentation or misuse of the law. There is no registration of guns in Pennsylvania, but nearly all sales and transfers are required to be recorded by a Federal Firearms Licensed dealer. Pennsylvania has concealed-carry reciprocity with approximately forty states, but that is subject to change. The attorney general of Pennsylvania is charged with negotiating and maintaining this reciprocity.

The message that was reiterated numerous times during the meeting was to be a responsible gun owner. Responsibilities extended into three areas: be trained in your firearm, know the law, and be prepared mentally and emotionally for the potential consequences of discharging your firearm. Firearms training should be continuous and multifaceted, such that the owner knows his or her firearms well, maintains them in good working order as well as loads and discharges them, and fires them frequently enough to be comfortable with their use. Knowledge of the law starts with being familiar with the contents of the summary book provided by the legislator.

Mental and emotional preparation includes understanding how Pennsylvania interprets individual rights. Citizens have a right to use a firearm to defend themselves and others in their home or car against unlawful intrusion or attack. A Pennsylvania resident also can "stand his ground and use force" outside his home or car if several specific conditions are met, including being under attack with a firearm or other deadly weapon such that it is reasonable to believe lethal force is immediately necessary to protect oneself against imminent death, serious injury, kidnapping, or rape. The person using lethal force cannot be engaged in criminal activity, must legally possess the firearm, and must not stop a law enforcement officer in performance of his or her duties. If all of these conditions are not met, the citizen has a duty to retreat. Once the threat to self is no longer imminent, the citizen must stand down and leave resolution of any larger issue to law enforcement personnel. If a citizen uses force

in accordance with the law, he or she may still face civil lawsuits by the attacker or the attacker's family. However, if that
citizen wins the lawsuit, he or she is protected by law and is
allowed to recover costs, fees, and lost income.

An emotionally based decision could easily put any
gun owner at risk of overstepping legal bounds. An action
like the armed engagement by a civilian neighbor with the
shooter at the church in Sutherland Springs, Texas, in
2017, would be considered a crime in Pennsylvania, since
the neighbor's life was not in danger. If we observe a shooting or other armed crime within Pennsylvania, the best
action is to call 911 and be the best witness we can be. We
are cautioned not to insert ourselves into potentially life-
threatening situations.

Florida's stand-your-ground law is different from
either Pennsylvania's or Texas's. We know of the Florida
law primarily due to two publicized shootings of Black teen-
agers: Trayvon Martin and Jordan Davis. In February 2012,
Trayvon Martin was visiting relatives in a gated community
when he was seen by George Zimmerman, a neighborhood
watch coordinator. Zimmerman reported him to police as
a suspicious character. In spite of police advice, Zimmerman followed Martin and a fight ensued. Martin was fatally
shot. Zimmerman claimed he feared for his life and that he
"stood his ground" by using lethal force. Zimmerman was
tried for murder but found not guilty. Jordan Davis was at a
gas station in November 2012 with three friends. The loud
music coming from their car annoyed Michael Dunn, who
was in an adjacent vehicle. He asked them to turn it down,
and they initially complied. When Davis complained and
they turned the volume back up, Dunn took his gun and
shot at the teens through their car door. Davis died from his
wounds. Dunn also used the stand-your-ground defense;

however, he did not call police prior to or immediately following the shooting. Dunn was tried twice: at the end of the first trial he was found guilty of three counts of attempted murder, and at the end of the second trial he was found guilty of the murder of Jordan Davis.

Each state has different laws. Details of federal and state gun laws and court decisions are available on the Web. You may want to reach out to a local legislator to explore your state laws related to firearms and learn where he or she stands. Due to the current climate of activism, we also can't assume that gun laws at any level remain the same from year to year.

THE CAR COMPARISON

I grew up in a different era, an era in which many young people died in car accidents. Some deaths were not so much accidents as consequences of the foolishness of youth. We liked to drive fast. One of my town's longest straight stretches of road ended with a curve—dead man's curve. Back then, many towns had one. That's what made Jan and Dean's song "Dead Man's Curve" so popular. We all could identify with it.

That was before problems with gas tanks in Ford Pintos bursting into flame on impact, before Chevy Corvairs with their rollover problems, and before Ralph Nader wrote *Unsafe at Any Speed*. As a result of Nader's book and multiple lawsuits against automobile manufacturers, Congress held hearings and passed new laws. Manufacturers were mandated to make safer cars.

The "nut behind the wheel" was no longer blamed for every fatality. Instead, door latches were improved and seat belts were added so people no longer would be thrown free from cars going sixty miles per hour. Steering columns became collapsible so drivers no longer would be impaled in a front-end collision. Suspensions were improved and gas tanks moved to relatively safe and secure positions. Cars have undergone a complete redesign from heavy, rigid vehicles to light, flexible ones that create a protective cocoon for their occupants upon impact. Cars now carry "black boxes" that automatically record data—including speed, acceleration, and deceleration—that are valuable forensic tools in evaluating fatal crashes.

I'm still a car person. I appreciate the feel of a sports car as it hugs the ground around corners. I like looking under the hood of a 1957 Chevy or a 1965 Mustang. Similarly, I appreciate the love gun owners have for guns. We can customize guns to fit our individual measurements and preferences. We can collect guns of a particular manufacturer, style, or vintage. We appreciate the sense of power that a gun gives, whether it's putting holes in a target, plinking a can or bottle, or setting off some Tannerite. We can't help but acknowledge, however, the power that both cars and guns have to cause injury or death. And that's the purpose of safety regulations.

As the automobile became a preferred method of transportation, federal legislation was instituted at various times to standardize certain aspects of vehicles and rules of the road. Often these laws came with offers of federal funds to support the growth of the auto industry and to gain support from the states. Those laws were augmented by state laws, but federal oversight has allowed standardization.

Imagine if we didn't have that federal oversight. In order to drive outside of Pennsylvania, I would have to make sure I understood the laws of every state I intended to drive through. I'd have to check to see if those states recognized the driver's license I received in Pennsylvania. Now, I only have to transfer my license when I take up residency in another state. A license issued in one state allows me to drive in all states. Getting a license involves both knowledge of the state motor vehicle laws and demonstrated safe practical experience in driving.

I own more than one car, and no one questions my "need" to have any particular car (except my wife sometimes). I have a car that I regularly use daily. In order to use it in public I need to have a current state license for myself and a current registration for the vehicle. To get the vehicle registered, I need to prove it is mine by producing a title for it. The title is tied to a unique identification number on the vehicle. I also have to demonstrate financial responsibility for what happens while I am driving the car in public. This is in the form of insurance against personal injury and property damage. I have to make sure the vehicle I drive is roadworthy by submitting it to periodic independent inspections. Similarly, if I am caught violating motor vehicle laws, I can be required to attend special classes or forfeit my license.

Classic and antique cars follow less stringent rules for registration, but the owner accepts more responsibility for their public use. Since I live on a farmstead, I have a couple of cars, "old beaters," that I use just on my own private property. They are not registered or insured, and I'm not sure I could produce a title for them. I know firsthand that licensing and registration of drivers and automobiles has not stopped people from legally, within limits, owning unregistered vehicles or driving them without a license. Since government regulation does not interfere with what I can do with and to cars in private, it is financial cost (not government infringement) that determines whether I own or modify a vehicle. I think the federal government's involvement with cars is balanced, sorting out my public responsibilities and my private rights.

There are groups of car owners concerned about federal oversight, and groups that monitor pending motor vehicle legislation and lobby on behalf of the car culture that is still strong in America. While car ownership is not an enshrined right, recent American history has demonstrated how we all benefit when manufacturers and owners work with legislatures to improve safety and require individual responsibility. It is now possible for some to dream of a time when we will not have any motor vehicle fatalities in America.

I can't help but draw parallels between our car culture and our gun culture. When I look at the success of preventing violent deaths and injuries from cars without significantly affecting my privilege of owning and using cars, I can't help but imagine how things could change if we adopted a similar approach to our guns. Think about how much could apply to both as we seek to reduce the incidence of injury and death from firearms. Passionate gun owners are naturally inclined to look away from guns as a cause of gun violence and gun deaths, but just as car manufacturers and enthusiasts conceded that there was more to automobile safety than the "nut behind the wheel," we need to concede that guns are one very violent way "people kill people." Guns do kill people.

MENTAL HEALTH AND GUN VIOLENCE

After every mass shooting, conversations seem to dissolve into debates over whether the shooter's mental state or access to guns is more to blame. I see this as a distraction to avoid addressing either part: the person or the gun. "Mental state" is not a precise term, any more than "mentally deficient." However, in most mass shootings there is a mental health component. Often it is detectable by others around the shooter in the days and weeks before the event. Sandy Hook Promise has a program to help teachers and staff "know the signs" when working with children and adolescents. For us adults, it's our responsibility. Unfortunately, we typically are in denial that there is any problem, so we don't act. People seem nearly as fearful of talking about mental health as they are about guns. But if we have a concern, we need to go to the source and voice it.

My wife struggles from time to time with depression. One time after she was voluntarily admitted to a psychiatric hospital for her own safety, I was asked if I had any guns in our house. When I said yes, I was told that I would need to affirm they were no longer in our house at the time of her release. This is because suicide by firearm is by far the most successful method. I know from personal experience that we can't remove everything with the potential for self-harm from mentally ill people and still ask them to navigate the mainstream of everyday life. But we still can help them avoid exposure to the most lethal weapons. It just makes sense not to allow them access to guns.

When my wife was discharged from the hospital, I was not asked what I had done with my guns. I wondered if they had the right to make that demand of me. There are other options, such as a gun safe, besides just removing guns from the house. I also wondered what it would be like to be tested like that. What if I had to choose between my wife and my guns? It seemed to me to be an unfair statement of the problem, and fodder for jokes.

Obviously, a primary goal of friends and family of someone with mental illness (and especially depression) is to help keep that person safe. First and foremost, that means not allowing them access to any type of firearm. If that person has never had a firearm, that task is somewhat easier. If that person owns firearms and likes shooting them, that is a problem. The shooter at Sandy Hook is a prime example of this. His mother enjoyed the social interaction she had with her son while shooting together. She thought she had things under control by locking the rifles in a gun safe. But all her son needed to do was keep one loaded gun out, shoot her, get the key, and raid the gun safe before he went to the school.

In a situation where the relationship with an intimate partner becomes violent or abusive, "Are there guns in the house?" also becomes one of the right questions. If the abuser won't take steps to remove guns from his life while he works on his anger management, the victim will have to decide whether to leave the abuser and his guns for her own self-preservation. If the victim leaves, there is always fear of retribution, and a restraining order is often sought from a court. It can help if the judge has the legal authority to have the guns removed from the abuser's control as long as the order is in effect.

Both mental illness and life crisis can lead to gun violence. Where intimate partners or family members are involved there can be combined murder-suicide. This is common enough to warrant a separate class of violent deaths in the CDC-NVDRS data.

GUNS AND THE MENTAL HEALTH OF VETERANS

Being shot or seeing people being shot is traumatic. Shooting other people is also traumatic. It has been through studies of soldiers in various wars that we have come to appreciate the complexity of posttraumatic stress disorder (PTSD), a form of mental illness. Lt. Col. Dave Grossman has documented some of this in his book *On Killing*. He states that somewhere between 500,000 and 1,500,000 Vietnam veterans have suffered from PTSD.[7] At the same time, he presents the case that most people strongly resist shooting at other people. He found that the firing rate of soldiers in combat rose from only 15 percent during World War II to 55 percent during the Korean War, to 90 percent or more during the Vietnam War.[8] Grossman argues that we should have reservations about the techniques used to make our soldiers such killing machines. He then turns from our military to our general society and finds essentially the same forces and factors at work to enable killing in America. These include the role of gangs in authorizing and absolving killings, desensitization and violent role models through media, video game conditioning, and the ability to put physical distance (through guns) and emotional distance (through class, racism, and poverty) between the shooter and his victim(s).[9] This summary acknowledges that the actual factors at work in any specific instance are complex, but Grossman sees America's indiscriminate application of killing-enabling processes as an alarming threat to the emotional health of our children.[10]

REFLECTION AND CONVERSATION

Approaches to gun violence in America are practically unlimited. This chapter only provides a sampling. In most cases, the first step can be simply performing an internet search on what you particularly want to explore. Take some time to think about guns and gun violence, and discuss the possibilities.

1. Do you lean toward gun rights or gun control? Are you involved with any of the groups mentioned in this chapter?

2. How do you see the relationship between guns and violence? Should we attempt to separate gun control and gun violence prevention, or are the two inexorably linked? What do you believe would reduce gun violence in America?

3. Should we use data and statistics to bolster claims related to guns and gun violence? Under what circumstances? Did any of the data presented in this chapter surprise you?

4. Do you know the laws governing gun ownership and use in your state? Do you think they are appropriate, or are there changes you would advocate? How much effort should we spend continuing to argue aspects of law that now appear to be settled?

5. What other areas related to guns and gun violence would you like to explore? Is there another point of comparison besides automobiles that you find especially relevant to the issue of gun violence, or another dimension besides mental health you want to discuss with a group or research on your own?

Chapter 4

VIOLENCE AND THE BIBLE

Reflecting on the issue of gun violence as people of faith, we turn to the Bible for guidance. Clearly, the weapons used in the Bible are not the firearms, guns, rifles, and explosives we have today, but as in all eras of world history, there were plenty of weapons with which to injure and kill. In the Bible, we find armies with archers, spearmen, and swordsmen. Those in power use stoning, hanging, feeding to wild beasts, and crucifixion as violent means to exert control over society. It seems just about anything could be considered to be a weapon in the Bible: even the jawbone of a donkey and a tent peg.

As Christians, we seek to apply the Bible's wisdom to our modern context, despite vast cultural differences. There was no internet in the Bible, for example, but we can still look to the Bible's guidance for our online behavior. In the same way, the Bible can give us insight with which to approach the issues surrounding modern guns and gun violence.

APPROACHING THE BIBLE

We begin our consideration of the Bible as we did with the topic of guns—by reflecting on how we came to know what we know about the Bible and how that has shaped us. Only then can we start to think about what we know about violence in the Bible and what that might tell us about gun violence today.

As a young adult, I didn't set out to become an ordained Christian minister. I was happy in my career as a scientist with an engineering company. I was involved in a local church. I was a deacon in my church. Then the minister left, setting off a season of conflict during which the congregation split along theological lines. The experience sent me off to seminary so I could get answers for myself. I wanted to learn enough Hebrew and Greek "to be dangerous" and interpret Scripture for myself. I quickly realized that I come to the Bible with my own filters, my own biases, my own perspectives, and my own prejudices. As much as I am able, I need to be aware of those. I know I can't totally divorce myself from them, but I need to own what is mine and what I bring to the Bible before I even read one word.

I approach the Bible as Scripture. I believe it *contains* God's Word, not that it *is* the infallible Word of God. I make this distinction because of my scientific background. I appreciate the scholarship of the past century that has applied natural, historical, linguistic, behavioral, and social science to our understanding of the texts before us. I appreciate that language itself is alive and that it changes over time. I appreciate that translation from any language to another language involves interpretation. I appreciate archaeology and the light it sheds on life in former times. I approach the Bible as ancient writings that still speak today—writings that are still holy, sacred, and special and that are set aside by the church precisely because God speaks through them.

WEAPONS AND VIOLENCE IN THE BIBLE

So what does the Bible say about violence—physical actions that cause injury and death—and about our responsibility to minimize such violence? Violent injury can be physically, emotionally, and spiritually abusive and oppressive. One of the Ten Commandments is "You shall not murder." The King James Version says, "Thou shalt not kill." The Hebrew word here doesn't exactly mean either murder or kill. It means to take a life outside of the sanctions of the government.[1] That killing could be either intentional or accidental. The commandment recognizes that the state has the power to take the lives of individuals under certain circumstances—for example, in the prosecution of justice, maintenance of order, or during war. People living under this commandment implicitly recognize the authority of the government to commit violence in the broad sense of the word.

By extension, the highest authority, God, can commit actions that we would consider violent in the prosecution of justice, the overthrow of oppression, the ending of abuse, or for other reasons that we individuals do not comprehend. This is not just an Old Testament idea. We cannot divide God. Paul, near the beginning of his letter to the Romans, says, "The wrath of God is revealed from heaven" (Rom. 1:18). When my seminary class was reading this passage from Romans in Greek, the professor quite calmly said, "Sooner or later, you will have to deal with the wrath of God."

Although I would like to see a simple movement away from violence as the Bible progresses, I don't see it. The Revelation to John is just as violent as Genesis. Violence is a reality we have to deal with throughout the Bible—however, there are different types of violence in the Bible, which can help us discern our own attitudes on violence. Certainly there is much violence of human against human and nation against nation in the Bible. It seems nothing much has changed over the centuries in that regard. However, the Bible also presents a God who does violence against people and nations. That is where we need to start as we seek to understand the moral dimensions of violence.

God is full of passion for his creation. At times that passion can appear as steadfast love full of mercy and grace. At other times, that passion appears as wrath in response to human failures. God is sovereign. God has his purposes, and uses whomever he chooses, whenever he chooses. Throughout the Bible we find not only a God of grace and salvation, but also a God of wrath and judgment. This God is One, showing us different facets of God's passionate love.

THE WRATH OF GOD

In his letter to the Romans, Paul indicates that God's wrath is revealed to humanity and all of creation. In Romans 1:18 and following, Paul presents wrath as God's response to a creation that ignores that revelation and does not honor or even acknowledge him. Paul says that God gives people up to "a debased mind and to things that should not be done." Those whom God gives up to these practices "deserve to die" and are condemned by the righteous judgment of God.

Within the Ten Commandments, the first commandments include "You shall have no other gods before me. . . . You shall not make for yourself an idol. . . . You shall not bow down to them or worship them; for I the LORD your

God am a jealous God." The word "jealous" has been used to describe God from the early English translations to today. It can also be translated "zealous." Both words reflect the essence of the root word: a hot passion for the object of one's love. That faithful passion can yield compassion, mercy, and grace. In the face of unfaithfulness on the part of the beloved, that passion can find expression in anger or wrath. This passion, this zeal, defines the relationship between God and God's people.

Before there was an Israelite nation or the law was given, God's passion for his creation—including people— was evident. In the beginning, God declared everything that he had created, including man and woman, to be very good. But also from the beginning, humanity has ignored God and God's counsel. We know the stories of Adam and Eve, Cain and Abel, and Noah. In the garden, Adam and Eve disobeyed God's instruction. As soon as there were siblings, there was a murder. Cain killed Abel in the fourth chapter of Genesis. God saw humankind's wickedness grow to the point where his wrath was provoked, so he covered the earth with a great flood. Only Noah and his family survived to carry on humankind.

The exodus story shows God at work during Israel's early history with Egypt. God hardened Pharaoh's heart and caused plagues to come upon Egypt, even to the death of first-born sons. When Pharaoh let the Israelites go but then chased them with his horses and chariots, God threw the Egyptian army into panic and terror. God drowned that army, and Israel saw it as a great work of the Lord. We recognize that Israel was oppressed and enslaved by Egypt and God was responding to their cries for justice. When reading about this conflict, it's easy to accept God's violence against Egypt as a matter of freedom and justice, but we can't deny that this story depicts God acting in zealous wrath.

During the time in the wilderness and through the conquest of the promised land, God's zeal for Israel is summarized as a promise in Exodus 15:11–18. There we read how the strength of God's zeal was to be felt by Israel's enemies as terror, trembling, dread, and dismay such that those enemies were powerless against the Israelites. We can find the details of this holy war most developed in Deuteronomy and Joshua, as God drove out the local peoples before the Israelites and banned the Israelites from interacting with people who worshiped other gods.

After the Israelites conquered the land and became established as a nation themselves, they too forgot God. In the third chapter of Micah, God declares, "Hear this, you rulers of the house of Jacob and chiefs of the house of Israel, who abhor justice and pervert all equity, who build Zion with blood and Jerusalem with wrong! . . . Therefore because of you Zion shall be plowed as a field; Jerusalem shall become a heap of ruins, and the mountain of the house a wooded height." In chapter 16 of Ezekiel, God spells out in graphic detail the abominations that Jerusalem has committed to warrant its destruction. There, God compares Israel to a woman cast aside at birth and rescued by God, who made a covenant with her. But she trusted in her own beauty and "played the whore," forgetting God and throwing away God's blessings. "Therefore," says verse 37, "I will gather all your lovers . . . against you from all around, and will uncover your nakedness to them, so that they may see all your nakedness."

Time and time again, the Israelites were disobedient and suffered under God's wrath until someone took action to turn away God's wrath by reestablishing justice.

Typically that person understood God's passion, God's zeal, and acted out of that passion. Phinehas is considered the prototypical zealot for God. His story is recorded in Numbers 25. A plague was affecting the Israelites, and it was determined to be due to people being led astray by local women and worshiping local gods. Just as Moses was telling leaders of the Israelites that they needed to kill anyone who had been led astray, one of the Israelites was seen with a local woman. Phinehas followed them and killed both the Israelite and the woman together on a single spear. God lifted the plague and declared that Phinehas had manifested God's zeal so fully on his behalf that he no longer felt the need to act against the Israelites. The book of Judges is a collection of similar stories of individuals acting as instruments of God's zeal—often in very violent ways.

As noted in Paul's letter to the Romans, God's wrath didn't end with the destruction of Jerusalem and ancient Israel. It continues throughout history to the end of time. In the Revelation to John, we find God the warrior recast as the militant Christ. We are forced to wrestle with gruesome, violent images as we read. Scholars have proposed various theories on how we might understand Revelation, and individual theories have been popular at different times over the past two thousand years. But the message is of God's wrath poured out.

MAKING SENSE OF VIOLENCE IN THE BIBLE

It can be hard to know what to do with these violent texts. So much blood is spilled in the Bible, and it seems that just as much ink has been spilled trying to help modern people make sense of it. In his book *Violence in Scripture,* Jerome

F. D. Creach sees God from the beginning as a nonviolent being, creating without the need for violent conflict. This is fundamental for his understanding of violence in the remainder of the Bible. Much of the violence has primarily symbolic meaning, Creach says, maintaining and protecting the "proper order in creation."[2] Exploring the concept of "seeking vengeance" through the prayers of God's people and the proclamations and practices of God's prophets, Creach concludes that prayer properly should call for the end of sin, not the destruction of sinners.[3] Expanding this, he also concludes that prophecy properly is not about punishment and the destruction of nations, but about the restoration and renewal of all nations as part of the kingdom of God through his mercy.[4]

I appreciate Creach's scholarship with respect to comparing the God of the Bible to other ancient gods, and I agree with him that God is free to do what God needs to do to maintain his creation. But while proper prayer and proper prophecy are admirable goals for us humans, the reality is that we are human and often fall short of what is right and proper. For me, his resolution of the issue of violence is too clean, cut, and dried. I find the Bible messy with violence from both God and humans, and I think we need to sit with that mess for a while to own our part of the problem.

For this reason, I find Philip Jenkins's *Laying Down the Sword: Why We Can't Ignore the Bible's Violent Verses* to be helpful. It provides a historical and sociological approach to the Bible and the Qur'an, looking at how Jews, Christians, and Muslims all read their scriptures selectively. He starts by correcting common misunderstandings about differences between the Bible and the Qur'an, noting that both scriptures have disturbing, violent passages as well as peaceful, comforting passages. We Christians tend to focus on the peaceful, comforting passages in our Bible and on the disturbing, violent passages in the Qur'an. To rectify this, he points to the conquest of the promised land as a series of "incredibly savage" massacres that are nowhere condemned or refuted in the Bible. Instead, he writes, "these events represent the foundations of later Biblical faith."[5]

This is a problem that we need to face, as we, too, have used Scripture to support violence. Jenkins points out that as Christian nations became empires, "chosenness gave divine authorization to subjugate and evict the former inhabitants of conquered lands."[6] Even before the United States could be considered an empire, Americans used that sense of chosenness to move from the Atlantic to the Pacific Ocean, claiming our promised land.

For Jenkins, the critical issue is not the bloodiness of Scriptures, but the methods we employ to interpret and use them. I agree that "the fact that a minority of activists derive harsh and violent ideas from the scriptures of Judaism, or any other faith, has no implications whatever for evaluating that religion, or the texts on which it is based."[7] Having admitted that these violent texts exist, we should consider how we are to deal with them. Jenkins reflects on various techniques that have been used in the past: avoiding them, editing them, spiritualizing them, interpreting them using allegory and analogy, and censoring or purging them. He concludes, "When all else has failed, the only way of dealing with these scriptures is to accept them, to acknowledge their existence, and to learn to live with them."[8]

He then suggests we learn to read scriptures whole and to explore their contexts. He recognizes that under particular circumstances, these texts may be used "to inspire and sacralize violence, to demonize opponents, and even to exalt the conflict to the level of cosmic war."[9] Those circumstances depend on conditions in governments and societies. If or when that religious violence occurs, it will be from the militant minority's use of the text and not the fault of the text itself.

Jenkins's approach really resonates with me. As I accept the whole of Scripture and see how it has been read and misread in the past, part of my challenge is to read and explore it fresh for today, without repeating those mistakes or introducing new ones. I can't help but be concerned that our reading of the Bible through the filter of a completely nonviolent God might introduce modern misinterpretations.

For example, the words of Isaiah 2:4b (repeated in Micah 4:3) are often proclaimed as evidence of God's opposition to violence: "They shall beat their swords into plowshares, and their spears into pruning hooks; nation shall not lift up sword against nation, neither shall they learn war anymore." Generally ignored are God's words to the prophet Joel regarding the time of final judgment: "Proclaim this among the nations: Prepare war, stir up the warriors. Let all the soldiers draw near, let them come up. Beat your plowshares into swords, and your pruning hooks into spears; let the weakling say, 'I am a warrior'" (Joel 3:9–10).

Context matters! In the first chapter of Isaiah, God declares doom: "I will pour out my wrath on my enemies, and avenge myself on my foes! . . . Zion shall be redeemed by justice, and those in her who repent, by righteousness. But rebels and sinners shall be destroyed together, and those who forsake the LORD shall be consumed" (Isa. 1:24b, 27–28). In response, Isaiah has a vision of the future, when all nations shall learn and walk in God's ways. It will be a time of judgment: "He shall judge between the nations, and shall arbitrate for many peoples; they shall beat their swords into plowshares, and their spears into pruning hooks; nation shall not lift up sword against nation, neither shall they learn war anymore." In Micah as well, this image looks past the present situation of the people's condemnation for their unfaithfulness and their wickedness to a time of justice and peace for all. It appears that justice and repentance are key.

Consider the Assyrians: a cruel, oppressive enemy of the Israelites. The prophet Jonah was told by God to "go at once to Nineveh" and cry out against it. Jonah didn't want to go, and that's when he got swallowed by that great fish. After that experience, Jonah did go to Nineveh and told its residents that they had forty days before they would be overthrown. The people repented, and God spared Nineveh. In response, Jonah said to God, "I knew that you are a gracious God and merciful, slow to anger, and abounding in steadfast love, and ready to relent from punishing." Jonah continued to carry his anger and could not accept the Ninevites' repentance as God had. This reminds me that my human anger must be different from God's anger in some way.

When I hear threats from God, I want to repent, return to God, and trust in God's mercy and grace. But being beloved of God while tending to ignore, disappoint, and frustrate that lover leads me into a dilemma. Like the Israelites of old, I'm prone to wander and forsake the God who loves me. Paul claims this as our common human dilemma (see Rom. 3:21–26; 7:14–25) and makes the case that God proposes a solution in the sacrifice of Jesus Christ. Jesus acted to turn away God's wrath. With this graceful action, we have peace, hope, and a new sense of the depth of God's love. This is the gospel of Christ for Paul. But that action, the sacrifice of Jesus, was itself extremely violent. A sacrifice is an act of offering something in place of something else. In a Christian context, Jesus Christ was offered, was killed, in place of each one of us who deserve to be put to death. We Christians claim that Jesus died once, for all, and put an end to holy sacrifice.

STUCK IN THE MIDDLE

While Paul can explain his understanding of how God works to resolve my dilemma, I still feel stuck in the middle of it. I find promises of God's success in the midst of my human failure as I read Psalms and Proverbs. Often those promises are in the form of pleas to God, to keep us on the right path, to teach us God's way, to deliver us from suffering and persecution, and to forgive us when we fail to keep faithful. Psalm 103 says the Lord "works vindication and justice for all who are oppressed," while also being compassionate, merciful, and gracious. I claim those for myself.

I hear Jesus teaching the Beatitudes and saying, "Blessed are the peacemakers, for they will be called children of God" (Matt. 5:9). I'm tempted to ignore a later verse in that same chapter: "You are the salt of the earth; but if salt has lost its taste, how can its saltiness be restored? It is no longer good for anything, but is thrown out and trampled under foot." The promise is there, along with a reminder of God's wrath. Luke 6 presents similar beatitudes and then continues with a list of woes—again a reminder of God's wrath.

In these same chapters, Jesus tells his followers to "love your enemies," "pray for those who persecute you"

(Matt. 5:44), and "do good to those who hate you" (Luke 6:27). Luke 6 also includes the saying "If anyone strikes you on the cheek, offer the other also" (Luke 6:29). Matthew's passage on love ends with the challenge "Be perfect, therefore, as your heavenly Father is perfect" (Matt. 5:48).

The core of the gospel is summed in two great commandments: love God and love your neighbor. They are presented in different settings in Matthew (22:34–40), Mark (12:28–34), and Luke (10:25–58). In each Gospel, Jesus makes a somewhat different point: all the law and the prophets hang on these two commandments (Matthew), they are much more important than burnt offerings and sacrifices (Mark), and in following them you will live (Luke). The Gospel of John has still another turn. In John 13:34 Jesus says, "I give you a new commandment, that you love one another. Just as I have loved you, you also should love one another." God loves us so much and abhors violence so much that God would rather die than inflict violence on us in spite of us doing the worst thing imaginable to God— killing God's son. As Jesus showed the depth of God's love in his death, we are challenged to show that same love through our lives.

RESPONDING TO THE VIOLENCE

There is plenty of violence in the Bible, and we don't get to cherry-pick only the verses we like to read. I have a dear old friend, a barren widow, who has lived a very complex life. A few years ago, she complained about the practice we find in the common lectionary and in other places of skipping over verses or ending readings early to avoid things that might be uncomfortable. She particularly does not like this practice applied to the Psalms. Many psalms include both blessings and curses, both joy and anger, both mercy and vengeance. We have to take the Bible, like life, in all its complexity, and make the best sense of it that we can.

I doubt that many of us would reject God because of the complexity of the Bible. We might be tempted, though, to imagine that our understanding of violence, especially God's violence, has evolved over time. We remember the Crusades and how Christians then thought the militant Christ would lead them to victory over infidels. We still struggle with evil, and the notion of evil people, evil communities, and evil nations. How are we to be zealous for God?

Philosopher René Girard proposed that cultures (societies and their particular religious underpinnings) developed as a result of the need to control our mimetic desires ("I want what you have. I want to be who you are."). This desire typically leads to rivalry and conflict. On the individual level, there is the story of Cain and Abel. With groups, that conflict shifts to violence (death or exclusion) against victims, as scapegoats. The origins of this collective violence are managed and concealed through prohibitions, rituals, and myths.[10] This pattern can be seen in many societies and their religions, and the ways they work together to maintain a sacred social order.

Based on this Girardian approach, James G. Williams says that the Bible offers glimpses of a God who abhors violence, a God who sides with victims. The Bible tells stories of struggles against human mimetic desire and struggles for good mimesis that we find most radically articulated in "the revelation in the story of the Innocent Victim."[11] Thus we can drastically reduce rivalry, conflict, and violence as our human mimetic desires are exposed by the good mimesis we see in Jesus, the Christ who was numbered with the transgressors.

In reflecting on America's historical faith-based underpinnings, Williams says, "I certainly think that witness to the God of the Scriptures is misguided if it seeks to assert the *chosenness, the special destiny* of a people as *superiority*, as inevitable triumph culturally and militarily over other nations."[12] This is the sacred social order we have uncritically accepted. He acknowledges that we also have a national sense of community care. We work to help others in need—the widow and the orphan, and those whose rights have been violated. "These two currents, the sacred social order and the unmasking of desire, violence, and sacrifice on behalf of the victims, intermingle in American traditions and in every aspect of American public and private life."[13] Williams continues by saying that this intermingling contributes to America's unique gun culture:

> The gun is a weapon whose ammunition can kill or maim, but the point is that its function is much like that of the amulet that wards off diseases and evil powers or the medicine that will prevent sickness and maintain one's health. In a world of rivalry run amok where people do not trust one another and where real dangers lurk, the gun is doubtless a kind of *pharmakon*, a remedy that is also a poison.[14]

It is clear that God sides with those who are victimized. I see Jesus as the ultimate innocent victim, whose death brought to light the depths of our violence toward each other. I also agree with Williams's assessment of America and its gun culture. As I look at our past, I see the role Christian interpretation has played in forging our "sacred"

American heritage. As I look at where we are now, when I keep my focus on the victims of violence, I find God. When I look to the perpetrators of violence, I find myself as one small, complicit part of a violent society.

BIBLE VIOLENCE AND GUN VIOLENCE

So what does this have to do with our discussion of modern gun violence? God is passionate and expresses anger. We humans are passionate, too. We may want to express our passion through violence. Is it ever right to use what we find in the Bible to justify violence? We can see through our study of both American history and Bible violence that Americans used Scripture to justify their conquests as the nation grew. That justification was not proper or appropriate, but it is a part of our past and we are still reaping the consequences of it. Are there ever times when evil needs to be faced with violence? Christians and non-Christians alike have always seemed to debate this. Practically from the beginning of warfare, there has been a "just war theory" to rationalize going to battle. However, exploration of "just war" is beyond the scope of this book.

Just as we have seen jihadists use the Qur'an to justify terrorism, within our own scriptures are the seeds for a militant minority of Christians to claim violence as a way to purge evil and redeem our nation. Following the model of Phinehas and his idolater/adulterer-penetrating spear in Numbers 25, they will use gun violence. We have already seen some of this, with numerous shootings at abortion clinics and Planned Parenthood centers by zealous Christians claiming to do God's will. Over eleven deaths were attributed to such attacks between 1993 and 2015.[15] This violence is wrong, follows an incomplete understanding of the Bible, and needs to be addressed.

As civility continues to unravel in America, such shootings—by Christians—become an increasing threat. It is easy to imagine other moral issues where a single militant zealot will decide someone has to do something to "make America right with God again." As American Christians, we must address such a simplistic understanding by promoting the study of violence in the Bible in all its complexity and wrestling openly with the issues we find there.

REFLECTION AND CONVERSATION

It may seem like this chapter has covered a lot, but it has only just scratched the surface of the topic. Take some quiet time to reflect on violence in the Bible. Think again about how you have approached the Bible, what filters you use when reading it, and how those filters influence the way you think about violence in the world.

1. How do you approach the Bible? To what extent does the Bible affect the way you live your life and view the world? Do all parts of the Bible have equal influence for you?

2. How do you feel about the violence in the Bible? Do you believe God is nonviolent, or do you think the idea of a nonviolent God is simply modern wishful thinking?

3. Can you see a difference between a nonviolent God and a God who abhors violence? How do you respond when faced with a situation where you may

have to do something you abhor? How do you think our human anger is different from God's anger?

4. Have you ever broken something or hurt someone in anger? Can our own love be strong enough to turn us from violence when we are angry? How does Jesus model that for us as we try to cultivate such a love?

5. God, cultures, communities, and individuals all play into our understanding of violence. Take a violent story from the Bible and see the interactions among these various "players." Where do authority, accountability, and responsibility rest, and how are they distributed among the players? Now take a story of gun violence from today's news and see who is involved, how, and why. Do the roles of authority, accountability, and responsibility appear to fall on appropriate players? Or are specific individuals or groups singled out to carry all the guilt?

6. How does love, God's love, become more than just a word spoken? How does it take concrete form and act with efficacy? Consider the models of Martin Luther King and Salvadoran archbishop Oscar Romero, both victims of gun violence, and look into their teachings. As we seek to love God and love our neighbor, what concrete actions can you and I take?

Chapter 5

TALKING ABOUT GUNS AS CHRISTIANS

Conversations about controversial topics can be scary. Bringing our faith to the table can make things even more challenging. Sharing a common faith and set of scriptures does not guarantee a common perspective, but ideally it will provide a framework of values and theological concerns to take into consideration. This chapter explores some of those theological issues that must be wrestled with as we think about guns and gun violence as Christians in America.

A QUESTION OF GOOD AND EVIL

One statement we all have heard is "It takes a good guy with a gun to stop a bad guy with a gun." This paints the issue as a case of us against them—"us" as completely good and "them" as completely evil. God made all things good, and yet "all have sinned and fall short of the glory of God," as Romans 3:23 says. None of us is perfect, and we all have the capacity to do bad things.

But we always look to divide people into camps. Life seems simpler if we have an "other" to hate. With rigid boundaries like that, it is very easy for me to dehumanize those on the other side. Really, they are just as human as I am. We both can say and do good things, but we also are prone to errors in judgment and even to doing harm to others. As soon as I dehumanize people, it is very easy for me to express hatred toward them, to respond in anger, or to condemn them. And then who's the "bad guy"?

As Christians, we are called to bless even those who curse us. The first step in blessing others is giving them respect as other human beings, even if that respect is not returned. This just starts the conversation.

A deeper question here is whether or not something intrinsically evil is fueling our violence and gun culture. If so, what might that be? In his classic *Moral Man and Immoral Society*, theologian and ethicist Reinhold Niebuhr showed how we can be prone to destructive tendencies as part of a group no matter how moral we think we are individually. So if we want to look at where evil might lurk, we should look to our organizations. And we should start at the top with our government, those who collectively control so much of our gun culture. Any group that is so prideful and arrogant that they do not willingly submit to critical scrutiny by others is in serious moral jeopardy. Those that refuse to heed the findings of that close scrutiny are headed for a fall.

We should remember that in the face of immoral groups and organizations, we can speak God's truth to power. In this way, we are providing critical scrutiny. Even if we do not change organizations, we can recognize and support individuals within those groups who come to claim their own moral agency as well.

ALLEGIANCE AND IDOLATRY

As American Christians, we must consider that there are areas where our values as Christians and our values as

Americans are at odds. This was brought to my attention especially in the days and months following 9/11. One Sunday that September, the minister at the church where I was a member at the time led the congregation in the Pledge of Allegiance during the children's message. It was met with a very positive response, and soon the congregation was reciting the Pledge during the middle of worship every Sunday. I saw a potential problem here. I had a talk with the minister, pointing out that worship is the time when we show our full and unrivaled allegiance to God, not to our nation. Not everyone in the congregation understood when we moved the Pledge to the greeting and announcement time before worship. Others would say it should not be recited in church on Sunday at all. When we hold strong allegiances to both God and nation, it can be easy to conflate the two, believing that loyalty to one is the same as loyalty to the other.

In his book *America and Its Guns*, James Atwood claims that guns have become our national idol, our golden calf. Idols are false gods in whom we invest power and trust to keep us well. Gun idolatry in America (which Atwood calls "Gundamentalism") is a well-developed belief system.[1] "Those who believe need guns to prove to themselves and others they are in control, to protect them from harm, and to give them a sense of security," he writes.[2] Guns are seen by many as "sacred" instruments, holding the power of life and death.

The Armor of Light is a documentary following two evangelicals as they wrestle with gun violence in America.[3] Lucy McBath is the mother of a Black teenage shooting victim who seeks justice and enlists the support of Robert Schenck. Schenck is a prolife advocate who was distressed when other prolife advocates turned to violence at abortion clinics. Much of the movie follows Schenck as he explores the gun culture within evangelical circles and finds his voice to speak out against gun violence. At one point in the movie, he challenges a group of evangelical Christians to consider that they hold the Bible as the final authority on everything but guns. For guns, they claim the Second Amendment to be the final authority. They do not see a problem with this dichotomy.

I know many Christians who believe America is that nation in a special relationship with God—the New Israel, as discussed in chapter 2. This can sometimes result in a belief that American laws are as God-ordained as the Ten Commandments. In his book *Bowing toward Babylon,* Craig Watts claims that our true idolatry is the placement of our American nation above God. We find security, identity, and meaning more in our national unity than in our Christianity. "When worship is infiltrated by patriotism or nationalism," Watts writes, "the door of the church ends up being opened wider for those who share in the love of country. But the door is unintentionally closed to those who do not share that particular love, regardless of their depth of Christian faith."[4]

As Christians in America, we need to ask ourselves this question: am I a Christian first, or an American first? I claim to be a Christian first and an American second, and I don't think that makes me unpatriotic. I'm someone who honors God over country. That means comparing my understanding of God in Christ to what I see and hear in America and calling things as I see them from that perspective. How this is applied to the issue of guns and gun violence may vary from Christian to Christian, but we should have in common our allegiance to God above all. Watts puts it this way:

Those of us living in America who are devoted to the one who came in vulnerability to practice self-less service and demonstrate nonviolent love reside in the mightiest nation the world has ever known, the Babylon of our time. . . . As a people defined by Jesus Christ we will not find our meaning in America and we will refuse to be enlisted in violent endeavors that insure American dominance at the expense of others. Instead we will . . . go into the world to reach across every wall of hostility with the determination to do good to all for whom Christ died.[5]

OUR BROTHER'S KEEPER

The Supreme Court's *Heller* decision made it clear that gun ownership is not an unrestricted right. It is "not a right to keep and carry any weapon whatsoever in any manner whatsoever and for whatever purpose."[6] Gun ownership is an individual right, but gun owners must be socially responsible for their guns. The right to bear arms does not extend into most government buildings, schools, or other sensitive places. A person can't carry a gun into a bank without repercussions. Dealers are prohibited from selling guns to felons and the mentally ill, and other laws may impose conditions and qualifications on the commercial sale of firearms. Similarly, the types of guns protected by the Second Amendment are those in common use and don't include unusual weapons such as machine guns and sawed-off shotguns. Owners, firearms dealers, and the weapons themselves all have restrictions in line with Second Amendment rights.

I like to ask gun owners to share the ways in which they are being responsible with their guns. I have always found this to be an enlightening conversation as long as I listen and don't pass judgment. If they have families with young children, they typically protect their children from the guns. It is becoming common for parents to ask the parents of their child's friends if they own any guns before allowing their child to go to those friends' houses. If they ask directly, they typically will receive a direct answer. Also if asked, gun owners will say exactly what precautions they take to keep everyone in the family safe. Gun safes and other types of locked storage are common precautions, as are trigger locks on weapons and separate storage of guns and ammunition. Some owners believe that knowledge and training are the keys to safety, and so they expose their children to proper use and care of firearms at a young age. We need to remember, however, that precautions on the part of gun owners are strictly voluntary. The level of care varies from individual to individual and from family to family.

The *Heller* decision allows individuals to maintain functional and loaded firearms in their home. Recognizing that handguns are the preferred firearm for self-defense within the home, it would be prudent to ask specifically if the parents have handguns, and not just guns in general. If the answer is yes, a reasonable follow-up conversation could include how the parents balance a desire for self-defense and a need to keep their children safe from handguns. Remember that children can be very inquisitive and discover all sorts of things parents have safely hidden away. If you as a parent are uncomfortable with answers you receive, simply don't allow your children into the gun owner's home. Share your decision with the gun owner as well as your children. The gun owner will understand and respect your decision, even if your children don't. If you as an adult are uncomfortable once you discover that other adults in your circle of friends are gun owners, possibly with concealed-carry permits and firearms in their homes, you can similarly share your concern with them. That disclosure will lead to great conversation.

These conversations can develop without stress if both parties are willing to listen as well as talk. Rather than getting defensive, do your part to be your brother's keeper by taking their concerns seriously. We can ask the questions and respond as mutually beloved by Christ. Ultimately, we all share in keeping each other safe.

LOVE CASTS OUT FEAR

I have said that we should approach each other as beloved of God. What I see, though, is that there seems to be much fear from everyone on the issue of guns and gun violence.

I see and hear fear from gun rights advocates: our Second Amendment rights are in danger, the government will know exactly what guns every individual has (so it can confiscate them any time it wants), and no one will have guns except criminals. I also see and hear fear from gun control advocates: no one needs a gun like that, bad guys start out as good guys, and the gun industry sells death. But these are just the fears we easily talk about. There are other fears deeper within all of us.

Those fears are about losing lives, losing our own lives or the lives of people we love. We don't want to talk about these fears. So we don't until it's too late and our loved one is gone. The gun deaths that make national news are the exceptions. Most of the time, only a few people hear the story. A first step in getting past our fear is naming it. Think about what you are afraid of when you hear about guns and gun violence. We seldom are afraid of abstract concepts or statistics. We are afraid that someone is going to come into our house looking for drug money and will kill us in the process. We are afraid that our neighbor has guns, we hear him shouting and screaming at his wife and kids, and we're just waiting for the night he goes over the edge. We are afraid we will just be in the wrong place at the wrong time and will be shot for no apparent reason. We feel powerless in our fears. We all do. But we all have choices.

I know that God is love, and there is no fear in perfect love. I wish I could just cast my fear into the sea. But my love is not perfect. What I cast upon the waters comes back again to me. Some of us look to reinforce our resolve to simply cast out fear through lucky charms: a plastic Jesus on the dashboard, a St. Christopher medal on our visor, or a rosary in our pocket. I confess I have a couple of rosaries, a few "saint" cards, and more than one plastic Jesus, even though I'm a Protestant. While they each in their way help my spiritual walk, they are not magical or lucky.

Others look to the security of a gun. Atwood says that America's gun culture (which he refers to as a "Gun Empire") uses fear to evangelize and win converts. In particular it draws on fear of the "other." While guns are purchased to provide safety and security, their presence reminds us of our fears. In addition, the presence of guns increases the risk of self-harm through accident or suicide. "When guns become idols and life seems too dangerous to be without them, one's ability to reason, cherish community, love neighbors, and depend on God for security are often surrendered," Atwood writes.[7] This is another way of saying once again that a gun is a remedy that we are willing to take in spite of its potentially lethal effects on ourselves and those around us.

How do we move from fear to love? For me, that movement starts as I remember the words of Jesus repeated in Matthew, Mark, and Luke: "For those who want to save their life will lose it, and those who lose their life for my sake will save it." This is right after Jesus says, "If any want to become my followers, let them deny themselves and take up their cross and follow me."

This passage speaks to me of yielding, not resisting. It speaks to me of looking past myself to others, and opening up myself to them. Nothing is as vulnerable as crucifixion. We all face death. We can work and work to provide stability and safety and security, but in the end we all die. Resistance is futile. Instead, I need to embrace the contingency of life and go forward yielded, open, and vulnerable. This is counter to the American way, counter to the way of the world. But it is a choice I make as a Christian. I make that choice again and again each time I talk or act on guns and gun violence.

FOSTERING COMPASSION

As Christians, we are called first and foremost to practice compassion—to see people in need and be moved to action. We are witnessing the impacts of increased gun violence—from friends deciding finally to purchase a handgun for protection to a pervading sense of hopelessness from living in a society that can turn into something like a war zone. What is a compassionate Christian response in the face of such violence?

We are familiar with human and child sacrifice from ancient cultures. I don't want my son or grandson to become some new, perverted kind of child sacrifice. I don't even want him to have to go through shooter response drills at school. We somehow got past the era of having duck-and-cover atomic bomb drills in school. We pray we can get past this as well. In the meantime, we can talk with children about the drills and listen to their fears. We can get the facts from local schools to see just what steps they are taking to keep everyone safe, and how they are dealing with the psychological impacts on the children while they are working to instill appropriate responses.

The violence of bullying is what Ronald Hecker Cram has called a spiritual crisis in our country. While we tend to think of bullying mostly as something that happens—and has been tolerated—during childhood, Cram's understanding is broader. He claims that "as adults, we have all been bullied and we have all bullied others."[8] He defines bullying very specifically as a behavior in which "an individual bully or a group of bullies seeks relation with another person or persons through repeated acts of violence over time."[9] Power is always a part of the dynamic of bullying. What we sometimes call domestic violence is a form of bullying. People who claim entitlement because of their perceived superiority practice bullying.

Bullying replaces God-centered relationships with violence-centered relationships. It is always destructive, to both the bully and the one bullied. When we add guns to violence-centered relationships, that destruction itself becomes even more violent: A wife and children are shot by an angry husband. A factory worker shoots his boss and coworkers before killing himself. A young boy who has been bullied relentlessly finds a gun and commits suicide.

Cram believes empathy is critical to addressing our crisis of bullying:

> Empathy is the essential core of hospitality, of the ability to recognize the "other" as fully human. . . . Hospitality is concerned with the integrity, mutuality, and the gift of diversity. With this recognition comes suffering. Where there is no empathy, there is no suffering in the presence of the other, there are the seeds of violence. Where there is no empathy, there can be no "other." Where there is no empathy, there can be no "self."[10]

He sees empathy as a way toward conversations that lead to conversions. The conversion that is necessary is one from hopelessness and its attendant fatalism: "the assumption that things cannot change . . . people cannot change . . . one is powerless to affect change."[11] Cram often sees this fatalism in the hearts of those bullied, and in addition he sees those people changed through acts of empathy. He offers a variety of ways to practice empathy: habitually being mindful of what is life-giving (empathy, hospitality, friendship, and caring) and what is not (injustice, prejudice, and hatred) in what we see and hear through our literature and media,[12] practicing the Christian virtues of faith, hope, and love (the moral life, with the gifts and fruits of the Holy Spirit),[13] writing a zero tolerance "bully policy" for your church or school, and inventorying empathy in worship.[14]

I think Cram is on target here. At its core, America's gun problem is really America's violence problem. Escalating gun violence is just one more sign we Americans face a crisis of violence. We Christians have the tools to speak to that violence and to walk along with others who suffer from it, too.

God sides with the poor, the weak, the broken, the lost, the captives, the blind, and the oppressed, essentially those typically on the fringes of society. Those trying to live on the fringes of society live by the Golden Rule: love your neighbor. At least that has been my experience, as far as I have seen and known them. They foster life, and they each have an important story to tell. That is why I do not dwell on statistics or numbers related to gun violence. Those numbers do not speak to life. People and their stories speak to life. That is why I want to hear people tell their stories. Even around instruments of death their stories have life. Each number represents a life, and that life is lost, devalued, and made insignificant in the great sea of numbers of individuals affected by gun violence. I think we need to move past the numbers and tell the stories. We all need to tell our own stories, not repeat stories we've heard. If we look with eyes that see and hear with ears that listen, we will see and hear Christ in the midst of these stories. That is what having a conversation is all about.

CONVERSATIONS AND CONGREGATIONS

When entering a conversation about guns and violence, I always stop to look around and see the context I'm in. There may be times when you may not want to engage in conversation, even on a topic like this that some of us can be quite passionate about. That's okay. Harmlessly deflect the lead. Don't go there. We can choose when to engage.

There are situations where it is perfectly fine not to take the bait and start talking about guns and violence. When the barber asks if I have anything planned for the weekend, I can choose to not tell her about a march or a protest I'm attending. It depends on how well I know the person with scissors next to my head, and how many others are in the room. Probably your family and friends have heard something from you about guns and gun violence. Mine certainly have. Most of mine tell me when they've heard enough. When I'm smart, I listen to them. Most of my gun-owning friends seem interested in talking and sharing good conversations about guns and gun violence.

As I enter into conversations about guns and gun violence, I need to be especially conscious of my reactions as others speak. My reactions may be related to fear, anger, or hatred. I need to name my emotions and own them. I don't necessarily need to share my emotions, but I don't want to simply react. I want to respond. I like to make a distinction between reacting and responding. When I react, my emotions are in control. When I respond, I have taken a second to process what I've heard so I can foster good conversation.

Where we live makes a difference. School districts throughout rural Pennsylvania declare an annual "Deer Day" to allow children to go hunting with their parents, but every day in the greater metropolitan Philadelphia and Pittsburgh areas, children shoot each other. This frames conversations about guns. Rural families see guns as one way to pass on family traditions. Urban families see guns as lethal weapons that tear families apart.

This doesn't mean we can't have conversations across the divide. I live in a rural area and am pretty sure there are multiple guns in most of the houses around me. I don't normally see or hear them, but from my conversations I know they are there. I have a good friend and colleague who pastors a congregation in a high-crime part of Pittsburgh. She has had to deal with the aftermath of shootings in her community. We have come together several times for mutual support over guns and gun violence prevention.

Talking about guns and violence in church can be especially dangerous if you expect more than "thoughts and prayers." When I first brought up the possibility of addressing gun violence in my home church, I quickly found out where some people stood. One of the first things I heard was "Guns don't kill people. People kill people." I also heard responses that were variations of "Neither do cars. Neither do airplanes. That hasn't stopped us from trying to make travel safer." But the middle of a church board meeting is not the time or place to respond directly to such comments. It's much better to offer a simple thank you and ask if others have something to share. Of course, at that point you might get someone else at the meeting who possesses a handgun and a permit offer to come Sunday mornings "prepared." Again, a simple "Thank you, we'll consider that" is sufficient before moving on.

I have heard of more than one Christian men's group in rural Pennsylvania who wanted to raise money for the church by having a dinner of game—venison, turkey, rabbit, and possibly squirrel—and then raffling off a hunting rifle after the dinner. This type of event is fairly common in rural areas, even in churches.

Before you start too many conversations at church, do a little homework. If your congregation is part of a denomination, convention, district, or other group of similar churches, check to see what is available through the records of the larger body. You may find something that your church has said or done about guns or gun violence. Ask clergy or other leaders to help you.

When I did this after the Sandy Hook Massacre, I went to the Christian Church (Disciples of Christ) website. I searched for ministries that might address the situation: the peace fellowship and family and youth services, among others. I searched to see if the denomination had passed any resolutions on guns or gun violence. It had, and those resolutions were framed in terms of "gun control." The last was a resolution from 1989 supporting the ban of automatic rifles. Prior to that, there was a resolution opposing gun control that was defeated in 1979, and a resolution calling for the ban of handguns in 1977. That was it.

I considered the Disciples statements and actions on the issue of gun violence altogether pitiful, especially when I also looked to see what sister denominations such as the United Church of Christ, the Presbyterian Church (U.S.A.), and the United Methodist Church had done and the resources they had available. If a search of your denomination's actions yields results similar to mine, be thankful we don't have to reinvent the wheel. Much has been done and is easily accessible. Remember to search other social issues such as domestic violence and bullying, as there may be resources of value there, too.

REFLECTION AND CONVERSATION

We have considered some hard topics here. Think back over this chapter, and identify those topics that gave you the most trouble. Maybe that trouble was felt as discomfort. Maybe it was a resistance to consider the topic, or an angle of the topic at hand that wasn't discussed. Maybe a particular angle on the issue arouses your passion and merits further research and work.

1. Do you believe there are "good guys" and "bad guys"? Especially when guns are involved, where might the lines between good and bad become

blurry? Can you imagine a circumstance in which a "good guy" could become a "bad guy"?

2. What responsibilities do we share as American Christians? Do you believe we are "our brother's keeper"? If so, in what ways? Do guns help or hinder our community well-being?

3. In what ways can our allegiance to country and the individual rights it protects conflict with our allegiance to Christ and our duty to practice compassion for others? How can we ensure that we are not venturing into idolatry?

4. How does fear usually manifest itself? What are healthy and unhealthy manifestations of fear? When thinking about guns and gun violence, what are you afraid of?

5. What were (or are) your experiences of bullying? In what ways are we teaching our children that bullying is okay, that violence is just another way to be in relation with someone? How can we encourage greater empathy and compassion in our families, congregations, and communities?

Chapter 6
BEYOND CONVERSATIONS

I hope that the discussions prompted by this book have been enlightening for you. But I also hope you want to do more than just talk. I certainly did as I learned more about guns and violence. With my priority as a Christian first, I started to tell my story to others, mainly to clergy and members within my denomination. Within a year of the Sandy Hook Massacre, I facilitated a workshop called "Can We Talk? Beginning Conversations about Guns and Gun Violence" for Disciples in Pennsylvania. Within that audience were representatives of the entire spectrum of positions on the issue, from a lifelong pacifist to an NRA life member. Everyone was interested in beginning conversations.

Our stories and perspectives aren't the same, but all are real, personal, and alive. None of our stories is ended. They are still developing and unfolding. As my story has unfolded, I have continued in prayerful discernment over my own steps forward. After that first workshop, my attention turned to formulating resolutions for consideration by Disciples, first within the Pennsylvania region and then within the general church. I researched formulation of resolutions within my denomination and reviewed resolutions on the topic of guns and gun violence put forth by other denominations. Some resolutions were very specific, while others were very broad. I sought guidance from those in leadership positions in the Disciples.

The best advice I received related to my approach. Would I simply tell my story and raise my concerns and trust the rest to God, or would I take the higher moral ground and advocate for a certain position? In other words, would I be willing to move beyond simple concern for the issue to speaking prophetically for social change? That question sent me to my knees in soul-searching and discernment.

The answer came from my story: who I am and where I have been. I confessed that I have been complicit in gun violence through my silence. I have seen that other Christian gun owners would accept the social responsibilities that come with ownership, even if they could not see themselves as complicit. I also have seen Christians who don't own guns urging that certain guns and gun accessories be banned. Both groups are Christians, and I need to meet both as Christ. And this old farm boy knows "you can lead a horse to water, but you can't make him drink." So I simply have done what I have discerned to be my calling and left the rest to God.

There were implications to this decision. First and foremost, my approach has put distance between me and those in the church who have been advocates for strong gun control. For me, the real issue is violence. Guns exacerbate violence. My focus has been violence prevention, and more specifically gun violence prevention. For me, this is different from gun control. While gun rights advocates agree that the issue is violence and that guns make things more violent, I find myself at odds with them when I start talking about ways we can responsibly help prevent violence, or at least reduce it. I believe responsible gun owners are responsible for controlling their guns, but time and time again I hear about unsecured guns being stolen, guns falling from concealed-carry holsters, and accidental discharges of firearms. And I hear or read about loaded guns left where inquisitive children can find and handle them.

Once I defined the issue as violence, I looked again at Jesus. He met violence with nonviolent grace. As his follower, can I model nonviolence in the face of violence? Again, part of the challenge is to identify violence I have done in all of its manifold forms. I have done violence to others primarily through words. In spite of the old saying that "sticks and stones can break my bones, but words will never hurt me," words do indeed hurt. I grew up teasing and being teased. I got quite good at it. It was a way I saw love and affection expressed within my family. As I grew up and out, I attempted to express affection to others through teasing—with nearly disastrous results.

As I have owned the violence I have done, I have found attempts to be nonviolent to be a continuing challenge, as my violence can be amazingly subtle. The subtlety of my violence was first brought to my attention in my seminary homiletics class. After I preached what I thought to be a strong sermon, the class critiqued it. One student said he found a statement I made to be "cutting." I no longer remember the statement, but I still hear his remark and remember that the class had a discussion about our duty to do no harm when we speak.

As much as I have had to accept God's grace for the violence I have committed, I need to acknowledge the grace God gives to others. I gracefully appreciate that God has called others to be prophetic in ways that I cannot. At the same time, I wonder how we as Christians can encourage gun owners to be more responsible.

RESOLVE AND RESOLUTIONS

Resolutions have been a popular mechanism to issue statements and promote change within several Protestant denominations. They have been a way for members and groups to bring concerns before the larger church. While some question the continued viability of resolutions, they do help at least those who assemble them.

I discerned that my denomination needed to address the issue of gun violence within both our regional and our general bodies. I looked at what other denominations had written so I could bring existing resolutions that I agreed with up to date and into sharper focus for my denomination. First, as the resolution for the Pennsylvania region was being developed, I shared versions and received suggestions from numerous reviewers and cosponsors. We ultimately developed nine clauses that we as Disciples believed summarized the reasons why we needed to address gun violence. Once the foundation was laid, we listed fourteen calls to action addressing the issue. Those calls included reflecting on our individual relationships with guns and sharing those reflections with each other, pondering our individual complicity and repenting of our hardness of heart, educating ourselves on guns and gun violence from a Christian perspective, taking informed Christian action on gun violence, and modeling grace-full anger management and nonviolent conflict resolution. Then, in 2015, through the work of others as well as the Pennsylvania region, a resolution on gun violence with eleven justifying clauses and six calls to action was adopted by our General Assembly.

Church resolutions can suffer the same fate as New Year's resolutions. Church members can agree upon social issues that need responses and vote to pass resolutions.

However, the will and the discipline to follow through can soon evaporate. Later, when the issue is revisited and previously identified responses have not been carried through, excuses may include insufficient staffing, insufficient funding, and competing needs. Nonetheless, I found great benefit in going through the process of putting down on paper why I believed actions should be taken and what form I thought those actions might take. Not all that I have hoped for around the issue of guns and gun violence has come to fruition within my denomination. There were disappointments as well as successes, but I continue to trust in the timing of God. There may be systems in place in your denominational tradition to draft resolutions or make statements about gun violence and our responses as Christians. Consider researching those and getting the conversation started on a higher level.

WORK IN LOCAL CONGREGATIONS

Within local churches, we don't all agree on social issues or how to handle them. When trying to engage the issue of gun violence, be careful not to coerce everyone to take a particular stance, but take a pragmatic approach to addressing real concerns in the community.

First, recognize that not all churches are automatically considered "gun-free zones." You can begin to raise the issue by discussing whether your congregation should decide formally that its property is a gun-free zone. I can easily imagine this will be a difficult question for many congregations. I'm prepared for those who would want to meet the prospect of violence with violence by carrying guns in church. It's important to me that church buildings are

sanctuaries, and that includes being a sanctuary from violence. Local law enforcement officials typically will share
their perspectives on the implications of knowing churches
and other properties claim gun-free status. Many busi-
nesses today declare themselves gun-free zones and deal
independently with the separate issue of security. We can
look through our community and to neighboring congregations to learn where local gun-free zones are found. That
will help us in our discernment and deliberations about the
firearms on church property.

Each congregation should have an emergency operations plan (EOP) in place, regardless of whether or not it
is gun free. The congregation should conduct periodic
reviews of the EOP. Response to an active shooter should
be part of this overall plan that also could include responses
to natural disasters such as wildfires and severe weather,
technological hazards such as power and water failures,
and other human threats such as arson or other violent acts.

The federal government offers an excellent resource,
*Guide for Developing High-Quality Emergency Operations
Plans for Houses of Worship*, that is available through the
Federal Emergency Management Agency (FEMA) for down-
load online.[1] This resource sets forth several key planning
principles: Planning should be supported by leadership.
Planning considers all threats and hazards. Planning considers all settings and all times. Planning provides for the access
and functional needs of the whole worshiping community. A
model EOP is created by following a collaborative process.[2]

The guide then lays out a six-step process for developing the plans. In many ways, going through the process
is as important as having a completed plan in place. It is
important to have the full support of the congregation as
you form a team that involves not only church leaders but

also community leaders, the local emergency management agency, and first responders. These other leaders are experienced in preparedness planning and can offer crucial guidance. At the completion of the plan, the local emergency management agency and first responders receive a copy to keep on file so that any response is coordinated. The plans typically define five areas—prevention, protection, mitigation, response, and recovery—but it is helpful to think simply of before, during, and after. Specific operations within the plan are separated into "functional annexes." These annexes may include evacuation, lockdown, shelter-in-place, recovery, and security. They may apply to multiple emergencies or be threat or hazard specific.

AN ACTIVE SHOOTER IN THE CHURCH

FEMA's guide takes a close look at active shooter situations. It covers both the responses of individuals and the responses of congregations. It is an unfortunate fact of life that today in America everyone needs to know how to respond in the presence of an active shooter. Just like we've been taught to "stop, drop, and roll" if we are ever on fire, we are now taught to "run, hide, or fight" if we ever face a shooter. If we hear the sound of gunshots (which often can sound like firecrackers), we should run away from the sound to a safe location. Each of us should occasionally visualize alternative escape routes from within buildings, depending on the threat's location. If running is not a safe option, we are instructed to hide in a location where we can lock and/or barricade a door, turn off lights, get out of sight, and remain silent until given an "all clear" by identifiable law enforcement. As a last resort, and if we sense we are in imminent danger, we are instructed to fight. A fire extinguisher, a chair, books, or anything else at hand can be used to disrupt and perhaps incapacitate the shooter. Finally, when first responders arrive, we are urged to cooperate fully. Remember that their first priority is to stop the shooter and secure the area. At this point, our job is to display empty hands with open palms and to follow any instructions given.[3]

Congregations can plan active-shooter prevention, reaction, and response operations. Specific plans are included in an "active shooter annex" to the overall EOP. As a result of working with local agencies and first responders, they will have advance information about the layout and details of buildings and grounds as well as other information that can prove invaluable in response to a shooting incident.

While not all shooters fit a standard profile, there are signs and indicators. These include a propensity for violent thoughts, feelings, and behaviors. These behaviors often include development of a personal grievance, recent acquisitions of multiple weapons, recent escalation in target practice and weapons training, recent interest in explosives, and intense interest or fascination with previous shootings or mass attacks.[4] Larger churches may consider organizing a threat assessment team (TAT) to receive and evaluate concerns and warning signs. "Often, violence may be prevented by identifying, assessing, and managing potential threats," FEMA's guide explains. "Recognizing these pre-attack warning signs and indicators might help disrupt a potentially tragic event."[5]

Unless they are retained by the congregation for security, assume that law enforcement officers will not be present at the start of the shooting. There is no single proper response; remember: "run-hide-fight." Since this is a sensitive but important topic, it would be valuable to have open conversations about it from time to time among members of the congregation.

After an incident is over and law enforcement declares the area secured, first responders will want to work with church leaders and congregants to transport the injured, interview witnesses, and initiate an investigation. It would be beneficial if an incident response team was already established, trained, and available to assist victims and their families. FEMA's guide describes why this is important: "While law enforcement and medical examiner procedures must be followed, families should receive accurate information as soon as possible. Having trained personnel to talk to loved ones about death and injury on hand or immediately available can ensure the notification is provided to family members with clarity and compassion."[6]

CHRISTIANS DOING AMERICAN CIVICS

As Christian Americans, we each have civic responsibilities, including voting to elect government officials to represent us. I know where my elected representatives stand on guns, gun violence prevention, and gun control. I let them know my position on pending legislation as appropriate. I have thanked them when they have taken what I think are responsible actions. There are watchdog groups who will alert followers of pending gun legislation. While I appreciate the notification, I prefer to send my own messages instead of responding to "click here" petitions or letters offered by these groups. Similarly, you may find a political action committee (PAC) that supports gun violence legislation in line with your understanding. A little time spent browsing on the internet will turn up prospects at both the state and federal levels. At the national level, I support the Giffords PAC, formerly Americans for Responsible Solutions, because its members' perspective as gun owners who accept their civic responsibilities aligns with my own.

The intensity of political involvement is a matter for individual discernment. You may sense a calling to interact with your legislators locally, to support a PAC, to lobby for political action against gun violence, or even to protest against inaction in the face of continued gun violence. There's an expression, "Stay in your lane," which basically means to find where you are comfortable and to do that. Others will act in other ways. Don't feel you need to suddenly change how you act politically (change lanes) as conditions appear to change on the issue.

In the face of those fearful of losing Second Amendment rights, remember that all Americans have First Amendment rights as well. Those rights include freedom of religion, freedom of speech, freedom of the press, freedom to assemble, and freedom to petition the government for redress of grievances. As a Christian, I value freedom as a source of creativity as I promote God's love. I don't want to abolish a legitimate freedom within the Second Amendment but to place it within the context of the other amendments.

At one point when I was consumed with zeal, I identified several legislative priorities for funding and repeal of relatively recent laws. These were initiatives on which I could track progress and for which I could advocate. They included:

- Increasing federal funding for the Bureau of Alcohol, Tobacco, Firearms, and Explosives (ATF) for prosecution of disreputable gun dealers who work with straw purchasers. Straw purchasers are people who purchase guns for individuals who can't legally purchase a gun themselves. A small percentage of Federal Firearms Licensed dealers apparently participate in such sales, even when the circumstances are obvious.

- Repealing laws that stand in the way of electronic record keeping. In this digital age, it is ludicrous that federal law forbids electronic record keeping of gun sales and transfers. The gun lobby is fearful that digital records of gun sales will lead to the government eventually knowing the whereabouts of all guns in America. They further fear that once the locations are known, the government could act to collect and confiscate them.

- Passing legislation to encourage and fund the collection of appropriate data from sources with the best knowledge of gun violence, including law enforcement and medical professionals. Funding for gun violence data collection now is essentially nonexistent.

- Passing legislation that encourages and funds best medical practices and protects medical professionals from reprisals if they publish papers to foster best practices in the treatment of victims of gun violence. Research and publication of best medical practices on gun trauma treatment within the health-care field currently is curtailed by intimidation and fear of loss of other federal medical research dollars.

- Repealing the special rights that weapons manufacturers and the gun industry have bought for themselves so that they are not held to even minimum product safety standards (as have been imposed on the auto industry) and are held immune to third-party class action lawsuits (as were successfully pursued against the tobacco industry).

- Repealing "open carry" legislation passed by several states. This fosters fear and intimidation, especially as citizens attempt to freely assemble, speak, and petition the government. It also is unequally enforced by authorities. Typically, privileged Whites are not questioned, while Blacks and other minorities are challenged when they attempt to carry weapons openly.

- Requiring minimum weapons training and examination for issuance of concealed-carry permits. Such permits are now available in all fifty states, with widely varying requirements.

- Removing "gag order" laws placed on physicians and mental health workers in some areas, which prevent them from discussing potential impacts of accessible guns with families and friends of domestic violence victims and individuals at strong risk of suicide.

This is just a quick list of a few critical systemic areas where I think prophetic Christian voices are needed to push for political change. On reflection, I find it telling that this list does not include legislation to control or ban any particular type of weapon or accessory. For me, focusing on gun control is like shooting ducks at a carnival booth. It looks and sounds easy, but ultimately we realize that others—that is, the NRA with its lobbying power—are in control of the outcome (at least for now). I see it as a distraction from other systemic work that needs to be done. You may see it differently and want to work specifically toward the ban or control of certain types of guns. If that is your passion and calling, do it. Start by learning about guns, their manufacturers, and the American gun industry. Do not advocate from a position of ignorance.

OTHER AVENUES OF ACTION

Just as guns and gun violence touch practically all aspects of American life, so does politics. However, there are avenues for action that don't directly require political action. Here is a sampling of issues that would benefit from informed Christian involvement.

Consider contributing to data and research. The federal government has identified data gaps and research needs. You could take the time to learn the types of data that are available and the additional types of data that would be beneficial in understanding guns and gun violence in America today. Among the many questions to be answered are: Who would be best suited for collection of this data, and what would be a proper format for its collection?

Consider focusing on policies around gun ownership. If you are a Christian who is also a gun owner, your input into this area would be especially valuable. The licensing of gun owners and the registration of firearms are among the most hotly contested issues related to gun violence. Gun owners already agree to licenses in order to pursue certain activities, such as hunting and concealed carry. Requirements such as citizenship, age, physical and mental abilities, written and practical examinations, and permit durations may be considered prior to licensing for gun ownership. I believe responsible gun ownership involves continual training and practice, and certain types of weapons require more training than others. I would like to see responsible Christian gun owners step forward to offer this, set within a Christian perspective. We all can share our own opinions and actions discerned through study and prayer.

Consider public health. Different types of guns create different types of wounds. Much of this has to do with the muzzle velocity of the gun. Different types of bullets create different types of wounds. The bullet may remain intact as it enters the body, or it may fragment, flatten, or otherwise increase internal damage. Doctors in trauma units need to know how to effectively treat the resultant variety of wounds. I admit I don't know the standard protocol when my local hospital treats gun victims, or how frequently it is employed. I know that doctors in America have always had to deal with gunshot wounds. I don't think medical practice has kept up with the technology of modern weaponry.

There are costs involved with all gun violence aspects of public health. These costs include spreading the knowledge and providing the training necessary for adequate and proper medical care. These costs include treatment costs for the victims, often including permanent disabilities and long-term care. Several estimates have been put forth, but further study and public awareness of these total costs to the nation are avenues for action.

Mental health is one specific aspect of public health. Organizations such as the National Alliance on Mental Illness (NAMI) address mental health and welcome active support. NAMI advocates for parity with physical health, for increased awareness, for better diagnosis and treatment, and for better lives for Americans dealing with mental illness. It seems that all groups want to overcome the stigma attached to mental illness. Nonetheless, there are special gun violence concerns of mentally ill people, their friends, and their families.

THE AFTERMATH OF GUN VIOLENCE

Any of us may find ourselves dealing with the aftermath of gun violence. It is always traumatic, whether there is one death or one hundred. In their book *Recovering from Un-Natural Disasters,* Laurie Kraus, David Holyan, and Bruce Wismer have adapted and expanded traditional grief-recovery natural-disaster-response models to address the added complications of violence and trauma on individuals and communities, with particular emphasis on communities of faith. They propose four phases from an old normal life to a new normal life, with pastoral care responses appropriate to each phase.[7]

The first phase is the initial reaction to the shattered community life: devastation and heroism. Usually there is an immediate rush to respond, to fix it, to make it all better. There is a heroic chaos of busyness until fatigue finally sets in. The most important things leaders can do during this time are breathe, breathe, and breathe. They are required to be nothing more than an honest and caring presence as they help shepherd the community through the chaos. They are to keep communication simple and accurate. As people find themselves in the valley of the shadow of death, they need connection and a chance to tell their stories to someone who will listen. The authors urge being wary of "what are sometimes referred to as 'SUVs': spontaneous uninvited volunteers. They will hear of the event and believe that they have a calling, a unique responsibility, or a special message to deliver to survivors and the traumatized community."[8] Newtown was flooded with such well-meaning people after the Sandy Hook shooting. Steer clear of these people! They are not helpful. During this time, the focus will be on feeling the intense pain and lamenting what has happened.

The second phase, disillusionment, begins as the heroic activities fade. This still is a downward movement, but it is not unhealthy. Kraus, Holyan, and Wismer claim that "it serves as a necessary corrective to denial or naive idealism. . . . A season of disillusionment is necessary to grow into the truths of the experience."[9] Acceptance of the trauma is the goal of this phase. That can come as the community continues telling the truths of the story, guarding against rumors and half-truths. The image of the valley of the shadow will shift to comparisons with the Israelites in exile or wandering in the desert. It is a time of deep reflection individually and in groups, comparing before and after. This is a time of vocational and missional searching, as what was before doesn't hold the same meaning now: "Embracing changes . . . in the months following trauma demonstrates belief in the power of resurrection; not to do so is a denial of its power in the midst of death; it is a turning away from the Holy Spirit who broods over chaos and brings creation out of nothing."[10]

The authors describe the phase when individuals and communities turn in the direction of hope as reforming, which they ground in the historical Protestant saying "Reformed, and always reforming." They relate this phase to chapter 3 of the book of Lamentations. After witnessing the destruction of Jerusalem and lamenting over it, that author shifts his focus in chapter 3, verse 21: "But this I call to mind, and therefore I have hope: The steadfast love of the LORD never ceases." The process of finding hope is uneven in all respects. Its pace and direction vary. Within any community there will be those who appear to get stuck or wander off. The journey from the valley of the shadow to new mercies every morning is what Kraus, Holyan, and Wismer call "a long and wearisome path to be trod,"[11] where holy, hard, and mysterious work must be done.

Recognizing the high cost of arriving at a new normal, Kraus, Holyan, and Wismer call the final phase wisdom. They do not attempt to describe what it entails but offer a few "wisdom markers," including a deeper acceptance and appreciation for our gifts, limitations, and failures, a new willingness to serve others through a mission or ministry informed by the trauma, and a more sustainable balance between work and self-care.[12]

FOLLOWING SOCIAL MEDIA

I have accumulated over two hundred links to websites relevant to guns and gun violence on my primary home computer, and I haven't automatically saved the link from every site I have visited. I have found that the same things that make the Web a good source can make it a poor source. The Web is current and fluid. As organizations grow, change, or die, a website that worked fine just a year ago might be obsolete this year. I have found that many organizations related to guns and gun violence have a political branch, and that branch may or may not be accessible at the same website.

The more I have been involved with this issue, the more I have grown in understanding. As my understanding has grown, my position on the issue has come into sharper focus. Over time, my personal focus has shifted from the focus of some organizations I had followed. Similarly, organizations undergo their own changes over time. An organization grows beyond expectations, its focus shifts, or it may cease to exist altogether. I have seen this firsthand.

After the Sandy Hook Massacre, the Web was inundated with new sites seeking to respond to gun violence. While most were legitimate and helpful, some promoted misinformation, including hoaxes and conspiracy theories, and others preyed on the desire of individuals to help from a distance, using fraud and deception. Similar responses can be expected with each new mass shooting. If you choose to get involved in this way, be diligent in checking a site before giving it too much personal data.

Among the many websites to emerge from Sandy Hook, I have followed three especially: the Newtown Alumni Fund (NAF), the Newtown Action Alliance (NAA), and the Sandy Hook Promise (SHP). The NAF was organized because alumni from the Newtown school system wanted to work with local organizations to help Newtown students and schools with longer-term needs after the initial attention wore off. As with the alumni of most other schools, Newtown alumni are scattered throughout America and the world. Some of us with close ties to Newtown refer to ourselves as part of the Newtown diaspora. This fund became a way for us to respond in a special way. Initially, the Newtown Rotary Club helped, serving as the 501(c)3 charitable organization receiving and dispersing gifts tagged for this local support. By February 2015, the Newtown Alumni Fund received its own 501(c)3 status, set up its own website, and maintained a Facebook group. Three years later, the website was down and the Facebook group was no longer current or active.

The Newtown Action Alliance started as a 501(c)3 charitable organization to help other people and communities going through what Newtown went through after a shooting. Its statement used to read, "The Newtown Action Alliance provides comfort, education, scholarship, and other support and resources to people and communities impacted by or living in the aftermath of gun violence in American society, and to help them lead the way toward positive cultural change." In addition to care for victims and their families, the NAA primarily provided support through linking with existing resources. This promoted cooperative advocacy and action and was successful enough that the group decided to split into two sister organizations. The Newtown Foundation now carries the 501(c)3 status and original mission statement. The NAA has moved on as a national 501(c)4 issue advocacy organization. Its refined mission is "to achieve the steady and continuous reduction of gun violence through legislative and cultural changes." Its primary focus is now to advocate for smarter, safer gun laws.

The Sandy Hook Promise emerged out of the grief of family members who had lost loved ones in the Sandy Hook Massacre. At first it was mostly a promise to transform the deaths at Sandy Hook into something good. Celebrities joined the community in advancing this cause. In May 2013, Newtown Youth Voices visited activist and folk singer Pete Seeger at his home and recorded a YouTube video in which Seeger read the Promise and the Newtown Youth Voices sang "If I Had a Hammer."[13] In June, an event was held at Newtown Congregational Church to show commitment to Sandy Hook Promise and featured Peter Yarrow (of the singing group Peter, Paul and Mary), poet Martin Espada, singer Vaneese Thomas, and others. Other benefits were held, and a website was established that allowed people to join in support by making the Promise. (See appendix A for a long version of the Sandy Hook Promise.) I was an early Promise maker, and I would watch as the number of people making the Promise increased.

When that number hit 100,000 it was a celebrated milestone! The group obviously was gaining traction with a larger audience. As the organization started moving more toward action, it focused on youth in schools and community organizations. It therefore made sense to recruit volunteer Promise Leaders who would reach out within their own local communities. I signed on as a Promise Leader when that number was about two hundred.

Today Sandy Hook Promise is a national organization looking to strengthen its base. It has simplified the Promise people make: "I promise to do all I can to protect children from gun violence by encouraging and supporting solutions that create safer, healthier homes, schools, and communities." Over three million people have taken the Promise, and there are over 5,000 Promise Leaders working in local communities. Their primary approach is to develop and deliver mental health and wellness programs for use in schools and local youth organizations. As of early 2018, SHP has five programs that offer training in healthy social involvement, safety assessment and intervention skills, and suicide prevention. Sandy Hook Promise recognizes the need to advocate for state and federal policies and has established the Sandy Hook Foundation and Sandy Hook Promise Action Fund as its advocacy wing.

REFLECTION AND CONVERSATION

I hope you will use this book as a starting point for further wrestling with the issue of guns and gun violence in America. Pray about what God would have you say and do. Seek counsel from leaders in your church, and not just those extroverted activists. Continue reading and studying the Bible. Be socially aware, both locally and nationally. Research what really interests you. Resist evil and promote love. Accept that you will never be fully prepared for action, and trust the outcome of all you say and do to God.

Consider these final questions as you ponder what next steps you might take as an individual or group.

1. Are there actions you feel led to take in your local church to help respond to or prepare for the possibility of gun violence? What groups or policies does your congregation already have in place? What gaps do you see?

2. If your church is part of a denominational structure, to what extent have you gotten involved in denominational politics? Have you written—or even read—resolutions put forth by denominational bodies? Have you ever been a delegate to denominational meetings? Similarly, to what extent have you gotten involved in local, state, or national politics?

3. What laws or policies do you feel most interested in advocating for or against? How could you begin to get involved with that particular aspect of political action?

4. Having read about the aftermath of gun violence and other "unnatural disasters," how do you plan to respond the next time a traumatic event occurs in your community or elsewhere?

5. What insights have you gained from this study about guns and gun violence in America? Have your thoughts or actions changed as a result of a particular topic examined?

Appendix A
THE SANDY HOOK PROMISE

Our hearts are broken; our spirit is not. And it is with this knowledge that we are able to move forward with purpose and strength.

This is a Promise:

To truly honor the lives lost by turning our tragedy into a moment of transformation.

This is a Promise:

To be open to all possibilities. There is no agenda other than to make our community and our nation a safer, better place.

This is a Promise:

To have the conversations on all the issues. Conversations where listening is as important as speaking. Conversations where even those with the most opposing views can debate in good will.

This is a Promise:

To turn the conversation into actions. Things must change. This is the time.

This is a Promise:

We make to our precious children. Because each child, every human life is filled with promise, and though we continue to be filled with unbearable pain we choose love, belief, and hope instead of anger.

This is a Promise:

To do everything in our power to be remembered not as the town filled with grief and victims; but as the place where real change began.

Our hearts are broken; our spirit is not.

This is our Promise:

The Sandy Hook Promise.

RECOMMENDED RESOURCES

WEBSITES

Church Links

Episcopal Peace Fellowship gun violence prevention action
    group (epfnational.org/gun-violence-prevention-action
    -group): resources for prayer, study, and action
Presbyterian Church (U.S.A.) Peace Fellowship (www
    .presbypeacefellowship.org/gun-violence/resources#
    .VmeD6SifOfS): extensive resources

Government Links

CDC 1994 report (www.cdc.gov/mmwr/preview/mmwr
    html/00023655.htm): "Deaths Resulting from Firearm-
    and Motor-Vehicle-Related Injuries—United States,
    1968-1991"
Census Bureau quick facts site (www.census.gov/quick
    facts/fact/table/US/PST045217)
Connecticut State Police report of the December 14, 2012,
    Sandy Hook Massacre (cspsandyhookreport.ct.gov)
FEMA, June 2013 report (www.fema.gov/media-library
    /assets/documents/33007): *Guide for Developing*

High-Quality Emergency Operations Plans for Houses of Worship

Las Vegas Metropolitan Police Department preliminary investigative report of mass shooting, October 1, 2017 (www.lvmpd.com/en-us/Documents/1_October _FIT_Report_01-18-2018_Footnoted.pdf)

U.S. Department of Justice, Bureau of Justice Statistics special report on gun violence, 1993–2011 (www.bjs .gov/content/pub/pdf/fv9311.pdf)

Gun Control Links

Coalition to Stop Gun Violence (www.csgv.org)

Everytown for Gun Safety (everytown.org): a coalition of mayors, moms (and dads), and survivors working to end gun violence

Giffords (giffords.org): overcoming entrenched interests to enact common-sense solutions to protect communities from gun violence

National Gun Victims Action Council (www.gunvictims action.org): a force for sane gun laws

Newtown Action Alliance (www.newtownactionalliance .org): a grassroots organization working to achieve reduction of gun violence through legislative and cultural changes

Parents against Gun Violence (www.parentsagainstgun violence.com): a nonpartisan group advocating for better prevention of gun violence

Sandy Hook Promise (www.sandyhookpromise.org): offering gun violence prevention programs for schools and community youth organizations

Gun Rights Links

Citizens Committee for the Right to Keep and Bear Arms
(www.ccrkba.org)

Concealed Carry Nation (www.concealednation.org): promoting the importance of responsible and legal concealed carry in the United States

Guns (www.guns.com/about-us): independent web publication dedicated to covering anything and everything related to firearms and ammunition

Institute for Legislative Action (www.nraila.org): the political arm of the NRA

National Rifle Association (home.nra.org): the preeminent U.S. firearms owners' organization

National Shooting Sports Federation (www.nssf.org /news): firearms industry trade association

Second Amendment Foundation (www.saf.org): promoting understanding of our firearms heritage through educational and legal action programs

Other Links

American Academy of Pediatrics' recommendations for gun violence prevention (www.aap.org/en-us/advocacy -and-policy/federal-advocacy/Pages/AAPFederalGun ViolencePreventionRecommendationstoWhiteHouse .aspx)

American Bar Association Standing Committee on Gun Violence (www.americanbar.org/groups/committees /gun_violence)

Children's Defense Fund gun violence prevention policy priority (www.childrensdefense.org/policy/policy -priorities/gun-violence-prevention/)

Gun Violence Archive (www.gunviolencearchive.org): a nonprofit that seeks to accurately collect, check, and disseminate information on gun-related violence in the United States

DOCUMENTARY FILMS

Disney, Abigail, dir. and Kathleen Hughes, codirector. *The Armor of Light*. Fork Films, 2015 (https://www .armoroflightfilm.com).

Doblmeier, Martin, dir. *The Power of Forgiveness*. Journey Films, 2007 (http://firstrunfeatures.com/forgiveness dvd.html).

Kirk, Michael, dir. "Gunned Down: The Power of the NRA." *Frontline*. WGBH Educational Foundation, 2015 (https://www.pbs.org/wgbh/frontline/film/gunned -down/).

Moore, Michael, dir. *Bowling for Columbine*. Iconolatry Productions, Inc., and VIF Babelsberger Filmproduktion GmbH & Co. Zweite KG, 2002 (https://www.mgm .com/#/our-titles/252/Bowling-for-Columbine).

Snyder, Kim, dir. *Newtown*. Mile 22 LLC, 2016 (http:// newtownfilm.com).

BOOKS

Atwood, James E. *America and Its Guns: A Theological Expose*. Eugene, OR: Cascade Books, 2012.

Brueggemann, Walter. *Divine Presence amid Violence: Contextualizing the Book of Joshua*. Eugene, OR: Cascade Books, 2009.

————. *Truth Speaks to Power: The Countercultural Nature of Scripture*. Louisville, KY: Westminster John Knox Press, 2013.

Cram, Ronald Hecker. *Bullying: A Spiritual Crisis*. St. Louis: Chalice Press, 2003.

Creach, Jerome F. D. *Violence in Scripture*. Interpretation: Resources for the Use of Scripture in the Church. Louisville, KY: Westminster John Knox Press, 2013.

Girard, René. *The Scapegoat*. Translated by Yvonne Freccero. Baltimore: Johns Hopkins University Press, 1989.

————. *Violence and the Sacred*. Translated by Patrick Gregory. Baltimore: Johns Hopkins University Press, 1979.

Grossman, Dave. *On Killing: The Psychological Cost of Learning to Kill in War and Society*. Revised edition. New York: Little, Brown, 2009.

Jenkins, Philip. *Laying Down the Sword: Why We Can't Ignore the Bible's Violent Verses*. New York: HarperOne, 2011.

Johnson, Nicholas. *Negroes and the Gun: The Black Tradition of Arms*. Amherst, NY: Prometheus Press, 2014.

Kraus, Laurie, David Holyan, and Bruce Wismer. *Recovering from Un-natural Disasters: A Guide for Pastors and Congregations after Violence and Trauma*. Louisville, KY: Westminster John Knox Press, 2017.

National Research Council, Committee to Improve Research Information and Data on Firearms. *Firearms and Violence: A Critical Review*. Edited by Charles F. Wellford, John V. Pepper, and Carol V. Petrie. Washington, DC: National Academies Press, 2005.

Slotkin, Richard. *Gunfighter Nation: The Myth of the Frontier in Twentieth-Century America*. Norman: University of Oklahoma Press, 1998.

————. *Regeneration through Violence: The Mythology of the American Frontier, 1600–1860.* New York: HarperCollins, 1996.

Watts, Craig M. *Bowing toward Babylon: The Nationalistic Subversion of Christian Worship in America.* Eugene, OR: Cascade Books, 2017.

Williams, James G. *The Bible, Violence, and the Sacred: Liberation from the Myth of Sanctioned Violence.* Valley Forge, PA: Trinity Press International, 1994.

Wink, Walter. *The Powers That Be: Theology for a New Millennium.* New York: Galilee-Doubleday, 1998.

Winkler, Adam. *Gunfight: The Battle over the Right to Bear Arms in America.* New York: W. W. Norton & Co., 2011.

NOTES

CHAPTER 1: OWNING OUR STORIES ABOUT GUNS AND GUN VIOLENCE

1. The story presented here is a summary gleaned from Suzanna Gratia Hupp, *From Luby's to the Legislature: One Woman's Fight against Gun Control* (San Antonio, TX: Privateer Publications, 2010).

2. The story presented here is a summary gleaned from Gabrielle Giffords and Mark Kelly, *Enough: Our Fight to Keep America Safe from Gun Violence* (New York: Scribner, 2014).

3. Giffords and Kelly, *Enough,* 110.

CHAPTER 2: AMERICA'S CULTURE OF GUNS

1. For a list of nearly two hundred common phrases related to gun violence, see James E. Atwood, *America and Its Guns: A Theological Expose* (Eugene, OR: Cascade Books, 2012), 45–47.

2. "America's Gun Culture in 10 Charts," BBC, March 21, 2018, https://www.bbc.com/news/world-us-canada-41488081.

3. "Why Are Americans So Obsessed with Guns?," BBC, n.d., http://www.bbc.co.uk/guides/z3t2hv4#zs2wmnb.

4. Richard Slotkin, *Gunfighter Nation: The Myth of the Frontier in Twentieth-Century America* (Norman: University of Oklahoma Press, 1998), 11.

5. Richard Slotkin, *Regeneration through Violence: The Mythology of the American Frontier, 1600–1860* (New York: HarperCollins, 1996), 466–516.

6. Slotkin, *Gunfighter Nation*, 13.

7. For an extended discussion of the myth of redemptive violence, see Walter Wink, *The Powers That Be: Theology for a New Millennium* (New York: Galilee-Doubleday, 1998), 42–62.

8. David D. Lee, *Sergeant York: An American Hero* (Lexington: The University of Kentucky Press, 1985), 19–20.

9. Robert Jewett and John Shelton Lawrence, *Captain America and the Crusade against Evil: The Dilemma of Zealous Nationalism* (Grand Rapids: Wm. B. Eerdmans Publishing Co., 2003), 31–32.

10. John Wiley Nelson, *Your God Is Alive and Well and Appearing in Popular Culture* (Philadelphia: Westminster Press, 1976), 30.

11. Nelson, *Your God Is Alive and Well*, 23.

12. John G. Cawelti, *The Six-Gun Mystique Sequel* (Bowling Green, OH: Bowling Green State University Popular Press, 1999), 103.

13. Cawelti, *Six-Gun Mystique Sequel*, 100–101.

14. Adam Winkler, *Gunfight: The Battle over the Right to Bear Arms in America* (New York: W. W. Norton & Co., 2011), 132.

15. Nicholas Johnson, *Negroes and the Gun: The Black Tradition of Arms* (Amherst, NY: Prometheus Press, 2014), 58.

16. Winkler, *Gunfight*, 143.

17. Johnson, *Negroes and the Gun*, 97.

18. Winkler, *Gunfight*, 233.

19. Winkler, 231.

20. Winkler, 246–47.

21. Megan Cerullo, "Unarmed Black Man Shot to Death in Own Backyard after Police Mistake Cell Phone for Weapon," *(New York) Daily News*, March 20, 2018, http://www.nydaily news.com/news/national/unarmed-black-man-shot-death-back yard-article-1.3886562.

22. Nisha Chittal, "Cops Shoot and Kill Man Holding Toy Gun in Wal-Mart," *MSNBC*, August 9, 2014, updated August 13, 2014, http://www.msnbc.com/msnbc/cops-shoot-and-kill -man-holding-toy-gun-walmart

23. Chris Kyle, with Scott McEwen and Jim DeFelice, *American Sniper* (New York: William Morrow, 2012), 11.

24. Kyle, *American Sniper*, 306.

CHAPTER 3: GUNS AND GUN VIOLENCE IN AMERICA

1. Wikipedia has a chronological list of school shootings in the United States: https://en.wikipedia.org/wiki/List_ of_school_shootings_in_the_United_States. It is admittedly incomplete, but it is extensive and informative.

2. National Research Council, Committee to Improve Research Information and Data on Firearms, *Firearms and Violence: A Critical Review*. edited by Charles F. Wellford, John V. Pepper, and Carol V. Petrie (Washington, DC: National Academies Press, 2005), ix.

3. National Research Council, *Firearms and Violence*, 2.

4. "Deaths Resulting from Firearm- and Motor-Vehicle -Related Injuries—United States, 1968–1991," *Morbidity and Mortality Weekly Report* (CDC) 43, no. 3 (January 28, 1994): 37–42.

5. "America's Gun Culture in 10 Charts," BBC, March 21, 2018, https://www.bbc.com/news/world-us-canada-41488081.

6. "Guns," Gallup, https://news.gallup.com/poll/1645/guns .aspx.

7. Dave Grossman, *On Killing: The Psychological Cost of Learning to Kill in War and Society*, rev. ed. (New York: Little, Brown, 2009), 285.

8. Grossman, *On Killing*, 36.

9. Grossman, 308.

10. Grossman, 309.

CHAPTER 4: VIOLENCE AND THE BIBLE

1. Gerhard von Rad, *Deuteronomy: A Commentary* (Philadelphia: Westminster Press, 1966), 58–59.

2. Jerome F. D. Creach, *Violence in Scripture*, Interpretation: Resources for the Use of Scripture in the Church (Louisville, KY: Westminster John Knox Press, 2013), 46.

3. Creach, *Violence in Scripture*, 215.

4. Creach, 190–91.

5. Philip Jenkins, *Laying Down the Sword: Why We Can't Ignore the Bible's Violent Verses* (New York: HarperOne, 2011), 27.

6. Jenkins, *Laying Down the Sword,* 124.

7. Jenkins, 163.

8. Jenkins, 184.

9. Jenkins, 251.

10. James G. Williams, *The Bible, Violence, and the Sacred: Liberation from the Myth of Sanctioned Violence* (Valley Forge, PA: Trinity Press International, 1994), 13.

11. Williams, *The Bible, Violence, and the Sacred,* 30–31.

12. Williams, 241.

13. Williams, 243.

14. Williams, 252.

15. Liam Stack, "A Brief History of Deadly Attacks on Abortion Providers," *New York Times*, November 29, 2015, https://www.nytimes.com/interactive/2015/11/29/us/30abortion-clinic-violence.html.

CHAPTER 5: TALKING ABOUT GUNS AS CHRISTIANS

1. James E. Atwood, *America and Its Guns: A Theological Expose* (Eugene, OR: Cascade Books, 2012), 82. Atwood gives Rev. Rachel Smith credit for the term "Gundamentalism." He

considers this belief system a cult and subsequently has authored a book with that title.

2. Atwood, *America and Its Guns*, 22.

3. Abigail Disney, director, and Kathleen Hughes, codirector, *The Armor of Light* (Fork Films, 2015). See the film's website (https://www.armoroflightfilm.com) for Christian resources, including screening kits.

4. Craig M. Watts, *Bowing toward Babylon: The Nationalistic Subversion of Christian Worship in America* (Eugene, OR: Cascade Books, 2017), 27.

5. Watts, *Bowing toward Babylon,* 168.

6. *District of Columbia v. Heller*, 554 U.S. ___ (2008), 54.

7. Atwood, *America and Its Guns,* 116.

8. Ronald Hecker Cram, *Bullying: A Spiritual Crisis* (St. Louis: Chalice Press, 2003), 44.

9. Cram, *Bullying*, 48.

10. Cram, 61.

11. Cram, 65.

12. Cram, 90–91.

13. Cram, 86.

14. Cram, 77.

CHAPTER 6: BEYOND CONVERSATIONS

1. *Guide for Developing High-Quality Emergency Operations Plans for Houses of Worship*, FEMA, June 2013, https://www.fema.gov/media-library/assets/documents/33007.

2. *Developing High-Quality Emergency Operations Plans*, 3–4.

3. *Developing High-Quality Emergency Operations Plans*, 29–31.

4. *Developing High-Quality Emergency Operations Plans*, 26.

5. *Developing High-Quality Emergency Operations Plans*, 28.

6. *Developing High-Quality Emergency Operations Plans*, 32.

7. Laurie Kraus, David Holyan, and Bruce Wismer, *Recovering from Un-Natural Disasters: A Guide for Pastors and Congregations after Violence and Trauma* (Louisville, KY: Westminster John Knox Press, 2017), xiv.

8. Kraus, Holyan, and Wismer, *Recovering from Un-Natural Disasters*, 12.

9. Kraus, Holyan, and Wismer, 48.

10. Kraus, Holyan, and Wismer, 56.

11. Kraus, Holyan, and Wismer, 90.

12. Kraus, Holyan, and Wismer, 101–3.

13. Newtown Youth Voices and Pete Seeger, "If I Had a Hammer," filmed by Max Galassi, posted on YouTube by JDA Channel, May 27, 2013, https://www.youtube.com/watch?v =WvPEng8mYBY&feature=youtu.be. The reading of the Promise starts at 1:34 and is a very early version.

CPSIA information can be obtained
at www.ICGtesting.com
Printed in the USA
FFHW011533250219
50700469-56086FF